The MYSTERY FANcier

Volume 10, Number 3
Summer 1988

The Mystery Fancier

Volume 10, Number 3
Summer 1988

TABLE OF CONTENTS

The Mystery Fancier (USPS: 428–590) is edited and published by-monthly by Guy M. Townsend, 407 Jefferson Street, Madison, IN 47250; William F. Deeck, associate editor. Single copy price: $7.50.

SUBSCRIPTION RATES: Second–class mail, U.S. & Canada, $25.00 per year (6 issues); first–class mail, U.S. and Canada, $30.00; overseas surface mail, $25.00; overseas air mail, $35.00.   Overseas subscribers please pay in international money order, check drawn on U.S. bank, or currency; no checks drawn on foreign banks, please.

Mysteriously Speaking . . .

The two blank pages at the beginning and the six blank pages at the end of TMF 10:2 were not my idea. I instructed the printer to print 10:2 exactly as 10:1 had been printed. In 10:1, as in all issues of TMF, the table of contents was printed inside the front cover. The person to whom the paste-up was entrusted at the printer's neglected to observe this fact and proceeded to paste up the pages with the table of contents printed on the first inside page, thus necessitating an additional signature of eight pages. His (or her) supervisor caught the error before the copies were bound, and the TOC was then printed inside the front cover. Rather than scrap the entire print run, the printer inserted the blank signature, hence the blank pages front and back. Sorry about that. If they offend you, just razor them out.

This issue will go to the printer at the end of August and should be in the mail to you before the end of September. The next issue will come out just as soon as I get enough copy to fill it. I always try to get the last number of the year out on time, since that's the issue in which I ask you to send along your renewal checks. With the last issue, TMF reached the magic two-hundred-subscribers mark (though that number includes some non-paying subscribers) and, even though there is always some attrition at year's end, I intend to continue TMF through volume eleven and beyond. With the printing duties out of the way, and with Bill Deeck cheerfully doing the bulk of the typing, TMF is once again a lot of fun for me, and I'll keep at it as long as you folks are interested enough to continue to subscribe.

TMF 10:2 included an index to TMF 9, compiled by the indefatigable Bill Deeck. The issue you have in your hand includes an index to TMF 8, also by Bill, and TMF 10:4 will include Bill's index to TMF 6 and TMF 7. Bill thinks he will have an index to TMF 10 ready in time for 11:1, at which time the first ten volumes of TMF will be completely indexed (an index to the first five volumes appeared in TMF 6:3, copies of which are still available for $3.00, postpaid).

Bouchercon XIX will be held in San Diego this year, and if you haven't already registered you may as well forget about it. The cut-off point was reached in early June, which will come as a shock to those of us who are inclined to wait until the last minute to make our plans. There was a waiting list for cancellations, but the date for getting on it will have passed before you receive this issue. I was not planning to attend anyway, being convinced that the day I set foot in California will be the day that bizarre place chooses to slip into the Pacific Ocean, but I'd be a bit miffed about this had I wanted to attend.

Last issue I mentioned Perseverance Press in this column, and this time I'd like to mention the other leading small press mystery publisher, Cliffhanger Press (P.O. Box 29527, Oakland, CA 94604). I've commented on Cliffhanger before, not always positively; this time I've got good news. Cliffhanger continues to publish its titles in a quality, trade-paperback format, but it has now begun to issue them in hard covers as well, and at a price several dollars below the going rate for such books. The trade-paperback editions run about $8.95 each, while the hard cover editions, complete with dust jackets, sell for $13.95 or $14.95. I don't know how publisher Nancy Chirich is managing to make ends meet at these prices, but they are good news for those of us who blanch at the $16.95 to $19.95 prices which have become common in the past year or so. A flyer describing Cliffhanger's offer-ings—at least thirteen titles either already in print or scheduled to be in print by summer's end—is available for the asking.

Ellery Queen, Sports Fan

Joe R. Christopher

Between 1929 and 1971, Ellery Queen appeared as the
detective in thirty-two novels, six books of short stories,
about 337 radio dramas, eleven movies, three television
series, and a few comic books and other minor works.
Most of the novels and, so far as is known, all the short
stories were written by two cousins in collaboration—
Frederic Dannay and Manfred B. Lee. They also collaborated on many of the radio dramas—all the early ones.
They reinforced their readers' memories of the detective's
name by signing the books as by *Ellery Queen*. All this
is well known, although Queen's reputation has slightly
declined among average readers of mysteries since the
cousins died. But the fiction continues to reappear in
paperback, and *Ellery Queen's Mystery Magazine*—edited
for many years by Dannay—still appears.

The two cousins, non-practicing Jews—both born in
Brooklyn, although one grew up in rural upstate New
York—seem not to have been especially interested in most
sports—except baseball.[1] In Dannay's autobiographical
novel, *The Golden Summer* (published under the pseudonym of Daniel Nathan), he mentions, humorously, playing
baseball—surely he means softball—at Scout Camp when

---

[1] Francis M. Nevins, Jr., and Ray Stanich. *The
Sound of Detection: Ellery Queen's Adventures in Radio.*
Madison, Indiana: Brownstone Books, 1983, pp. 5, 77.

he was ten years old.[1]   The autobiographical figure,
Danny, also receives a child's baseball novel during a
week he is sick--along with a variety of other books.[2]
But Dannay also mentions, in one of his historical bridge
passages, the Jess Willard-Jack Johnson heavyweight
champion boxing fight in Havana, Cuba, "[e]arlier that
year,"[3] so Dannay may have had some interest in boxing--
a rather mixed interest, perhaps, as the boxing story
discussed in this paper will suggest.

However much or little Dannay and Lee were interested
in sports, they certainly were interested in selling fiction
and, therefore, in tying into the interests of the American
public.   They deliberately picked different settings as
their backgrounds in the early novels--a theater in *The
Roman Hat Mystery* (1929), their first; a department store
in *The French Powder Mystery* (1930); a hospital in *The
Dutch Shoe Mystery* (1931); and so on.   Because of this,
it is not surprising that *The American Gun Mystery* (1933)
is laid in a sports arena in New York City--although the
choice of a rodeo for the sport being presented *is*
surprising.   This novel also has a boxing subplot in its
center.   But boxing may have intrigued the cousins--at
least Dannay, as suggested above--more than most non-
baseball sports.   One of Queen's later short shorts, "A
Matter of Seconds" (1973, collected in *Queen's Bureau of
Investigation*), involves the kidnapping of a boxer.

But more interesting than the early and late boxing
fictions is a concern with sports which appeared in the
late 1930s and early 1940s.   Frederic Dannay edited, as
Queen's third thematic anthology of mystery fiction,
Sporting Blood: The Great Sports Detective Stories. This
appeared in 1942, but he must have been working on it
for a year or so before that.   Furthermore, three years
previously, in 1939 appeared four sports-mystery short
stories, collected the next year in *The "New" Adventures
of Ellery Queen.*   One of these four stories, "Mind over
Matter," was the boxing story referred to above which
suggests a mixed attitude towards the sport; and two of

---

[1] Daniel Nathan. *The Golden Summer.* Boston:
Little, Brown, 1953, pp. 124-127.

[2] *Ibid.,* p. 156.

[3] *Ibid.,* p. 155.

these stories were reprinted in the anthology two years later. Finally, in this same period, "The Adventure of the Swiss Nutcracker" was a radio script broadcast on 14 December 1939.[1] Although it was probably a Christmas show, and from the title probably involving echoes of *The Nutcracker Suite,* nevertheless it also involved the game of Ping-Pong.[2] No recording of the broadcast is known to have survived, and the script, if it still exists, has not been published; yet it is easy to imagine that the sound of the game of Ping-Pong would have been very effective over the radio.

It is with the four short stories of this sporting period in the career of Ellery Queen, detective, that the following comments are concerned, and to them this essay now turns.

The first of these four is "Man Bites Dog," first published in *Blue Book* magazine, June 1939.[3] For this baseball story, Queen invents an imaginary "New York series"[4]—that is, a seven-game World Series between the New York Giants and the New York Yankees. No year is given, but the story was probably inspired by the New York series of 1936 and 1937, although neither ran to seven games. There had also been New York series in 1921, 1922, and 1923; but they seem too early to be influential.

The story opens with Ellery in Hollywood, lamenting his absence from New York to Paula Paris, a gossip

---

[1] Nevins and Stanich, p. 94.

[2] Ellery Queen, ed. *Sporting Blood: The Great Sports Detective Stories.* Boston: Little, Brown, 1942, p. 246, a fact not noted in Nevins and Stanich. [The edition checked was the Blue Ribbon Books edition (Garden City, New York, 1946), a hardcover reprint which changed the title to the subtitle but used the original plates.]

[3] Francis M. Nevins, Jr. *Royal Bloodline: Ellery Queen, Author and Detective.* Bowling Green, Ohio: Bowling Green University Popular Press, 1974, p. 236.

[4] Ellery Queen. *The "New" Adventures of Ellery Queen, Including an Amazing Short Novel, "The Lamp of God."* New York: Frederick A. Stokes, 1940, p. 207.

columnist he was romantically involved with in two novels
and these four stories of the time:

> "Never missed a New York series before," wailed Mr.
> Queen. "Driving me cuckoo. And what a battle!
> Greatest series ever played. Moore and DiMaggio have
> done miracles in the outfield. Giants have pulled a
> triple play. Goofy Gomez struck out fourteen men to
> win the first game. Hubbell's pitched a one-hit
> shutout. And today Dickey came up in the ninth
> inning with the bases loaded, two out, and the Yanks
> three runs behind, and slammed a homer over the
> right-field stands!"[1]

Thus Ellery is established as a knowledgeable baseball
enthusiast. Paula Paris is used as a foil. After the above
paragraph,

> "Is that good?" asked Miss Paris.
> "Good!" howled Mr. Queen. "It merely sent the
> series into a seventh game."[2]

It seems unlikely that a Hollywood columnist would be this
naïve about baseball, but female ignorance has been used
elsewhere in popular fiction as an expository device. The
next story will reverse the roles.
　　After Ellery and Paula fly to New York, and Ellery's
father (an inspector of the New York police) wangles for
them a box behind the Yankee dugout, the emphasis on
the game continues as almost a counterpoint to the
murder plot. The exposition of the mystery plot is
interspersed with comments on the pre-game batting
practice. The actual death comes near the end of the
first inning. In this inning, the Yankees are at bat first,
with Carl Hubbell pitching for the Giants.[3] In the second
half of the inning, Gomez pitches for the Yankees. He
walks Jo-Jo Moore, strikes out Bartell, but gives up a
single to Jeep Ripple. At this point, one out, two on, Mel
Ott at bat, a man collapses (and later dies) from poison in

---

[1] *Ibid.*, pp. 207–208.

[2] *Ibid.*, p. 208.

[3] *Ibid.*, p. 216.

the box in front of Ellery.[1] By the third inning, Ellery is summoned by his father to help with the investigation in an office away from the game and presumably under the stands. Ellery solves the case and gets back to his box in the last of the ninth, with the score tied three to three. Bartell singles, Ripple sacrifices him to second. The story ends this way:

> ... Mr. Queen was already fiercely rapt in contemplation of Mel Ott's bat as it swung back and Señor Gomez's ball as it left the Señor's hand to streak towards the plate.[2]

The lack of decision in the ball game, as contrasted to the solution of the murder puzzle, is basic to the indication of the fascination of the game. The murder is an interruption, not tied to the game itself, although the man murdered is a retired ballplayer. The enjoyment of the game of skill, with small side bets between Sergeant Velie (of the New York police) and Ellery[3], is what is being celebrated in this story.

Two minor sporting matters may be added to these comments about "Man Bites Dog." Part of the background to the baseball game is the ballpark food. "Ellery filled his lap and Paula's with peanut hulls, consumed frankfurters and soda pop immoderately ...."[4]   Thus, it is appropriate that the murder, at first, seems to have occurred by means of a hot dog dosed with prussic acid.[5] The title of the story, instead of referring to the basis of news, refers to this hypothesis. As Sergeant Velie phrases it, "[His wife] poisoned his dog. Man bites dog, and--zowie."[6] The title is thus both a pun--*dog* in two senses--and a deliberate mislead for the reader. The real

---

[1] *Ibid.*

[2] *Ibid.*, p. 230.

[3] *Ibid.*, p.209.

[4] *Ibid.*, p. 208.

[5] *Ibid.*, pp. 219-220, 222.

[6] *Ibid.*, p. 220.

method of murder is a poisoned pencil which the ex-baseballer licks--evidently a habit--while signing a few autographs.[1] But signatures of baseball players are also part of the ballpark experience. The actual murder is more complicated, involving a young boy fan and other matters, but this is enough to suggest how Queen has taken a murder tied to a love quadrangle and integrated it into a baseball setting. It is well done, and it is appropriate that Francis M. Nevins, Jr., has called this one of Queen's eight best short fictions.[2]

An authorial point may be added to this story. The small boy who is involved in the murder case is one of the fans who gets the murder victim's autograph just before the game; he is referred to as "a little squirt in knee pants"[3] by an usher; later, the author describes him as "a boy with brown hair and quick, clever eyes."[4] What is significant is that his name is Fenimore Feigenspan.[5] He is never said to be Jewish, but the name all but proves that he is. Surely Dannay and Lee have written themselves into this story as the boy with clever eyes, as the Jewish boy, here from the Bronx,[6] instead of Brooklyn, who loves baseball.

The second of these four stories is "Long Shot," which was published in *Blue Book* magazine in September of 1939, three months after the first story appeared there.[7] The opening situation is that Ellery, writing for the movies, has been assigned to write a horseracing—mystery script. As Ellery explains to Paula, "I'm not interested in

---

[1] *Ibid.*, pp. 215, 224.

[2] Nevins, pp. 13–14.

[3] *"New" Adventures*, p. 221.

[4] *Ibid.*, p. 225.

[5] *Ibid.*

[6] *Ibid.*

[7] Nevins, p. 236.

racing. I've never even *seen* a race."[1] This allows Paula
to take Ellery to a California horse ranch. The plot is
complicated and, as Ellery comments, much like "a Class
B movie."[2] Essentially, John Scott, an "old" Scotsman[3]
with a young daughter and one good horse, must have
that horse, named Danger, win the $100,000 Santa Anita
Handicap the following Saturday, or he will lose his
ranch.[4] Santelli—one notices the Italian name—who is a
big-time bookie and who owns the biggest stable in the
West—shows up to offer Scott $100,000 for his small
stable.[5] It is notable that Nevins did *not* call this story
one of Queen's best.

Probably there is a good reason for this to sound like
a Class B movie. In one of the biographical sketches of
Dannay and Lee, this dialogue about their working in
Hollywood is reported:

> Lee: "Don't let anyone tell you that fantastic
> stories of Hollywood are exaggerated."
> Dannay: "They don't tell the half of it. Our
> first assignment was to do a racing story."
> Lee: "Neither of us had ever seen a horse race
> and we haven't yet."
> Dannay: "But we found a man who knew racing
> from the ground up, lived with him for three days
> and nights, and wrote the picture."
> Lee: "Which delighted the producer."[6]

If the cousins imitated their own ignorance of racing in
Ellery as detective, as they obviously have, then it would
not be surprising if they have also reproduced their un-
produced film script in this short story. Certainly, the

---

[1] *"New" Adventures,* p. 234.

[2] *Ibid.,* p. 235.

[3] *Ibid.,* p. 234.

[4] *Ibid.,* p. 235.

[5] *Ibid.,* pp. 235–236.

[6] *Current Biography, 1944,* quoted in Nevins and
Stanich, pp. 16–17.

material does not seem to have the same love-of-the-sport as the baseball story does, suggested by its celebration of players of the day.

However, there are some nice sporting passages anyway. The best description from the sports-fiction point of view comes just after Broomstick, Santelli's horse and the favorite in the race, is scratched because he has pulled a tendon:[1]

> "Here they come!"
> The shout shook the stands. A line of regal animals began to emerge from the paddock. Paula and Ellery rose with the other restless thousands, and craned. The Handicap contestants were parading to the post!
> There was *High Tor,* who had gone lame in the stretch at the Derby two years before and had not run a race since. This was to be his comeback; the insiders held him in contempt which the public apparently shared, for he was quoted at 50 to 1. There was little *Fighting Billy.* There was *Equator,* prancing sedately along with Buzz Hickey up. There was *Danger!* Glossy, black, gigantic, imperial, *Danger* was nervous. Whitey Williams [the jockey] was having a difficult time controlling him and a stablehand was struggling at his bit.[2]

Three exclamation points in this passage show the attempt on the part of Queen to capture the excitement of horse racing for aficionados. Parts of the plot also involve details of races—switched saddles at one point,[3] and certainly betting odds.[4] Some of this background is built in by having Ellery spend several days at the Scott ranch:

> He learned much about jockeys, touts, racing procedure, gear, handicaps, purses, forfeits,

---

[1] *"New" Adventures,* pp. 242-243.

[2] *Ibid.,* p. 243, with italics for horses' names as in book.

[3] *Ibid.,* pp. 246-247, 250-251.

[4] *Ibid.,* p. 248.

stewards, the way of bookmakers, famous races and
horses and owners and tracks....[1]

(The "several days"[2] match the three days and nights of
the cousins with their expert.) All of these aspects are
not given in later-developed details of the story, but
perhaps the generalized background can be taken as the
reason for Ellery leaping to his feet when the horses
come in and for him being able to later reason about
details of racing procedures.

The title of the story, "Long Shot," is of interest. It
has two basic meanings. First, after the daughter is
kidnapped, her wimpish boyfriend, following instructions
from the kidnappers in order to get Katie back,[3] stands
up in the stands at the race and fires a snub-nosed
automatic from fifty feet away, seemingly at John Scott;
Danger is hit.[4] Fifty feet with an automatic may be
considered a long shot, although with an experienced
gunsman it should be accurate; in this case, the person
shooting has no experience with guns. The second
meaning refers to the 50-to-1 odds against High Tor.
With Broomstick having pulled a tendon and with Danger
being shot, although not fatally--that is, with both of
them scratched--High Tor wins the race.[5] Ellery Queen,
the character, points out these two meanings.[6]

But, indeed, there may be a third meaning for the
title, for it is a decidedly long shot, in the metaphoric
sense, which arranges the happy ending--John Scott
retaining his ranch and Katie getting engaged to her
boyfriend.[7] This absurdity, acceptable only as part of
the comedic form of the detective story--or a Class B

---

[1] *Ibid.*, p. 239.

[2] *Ibid.*

[3] *Ibid.*, p. 252.

[4] *Ibid.*, p. 244.

[5] *Ibid.*, p. 245.

[6] *Ibid.*

[7] *Ibid.*, p. 253.

movie—is caused by the boyfriend, Hank Halliday, who was earlier kicked by John Scott, deciding not to bet on Danger in reaction and betting $2,000—"a little nest egg my mother left me," Halliday explains—on High Tor, because the horse had "such a beautiful name."[1]   In short, although there are a few nice touches from the world of horse racing, the reader was well warned about a B-movie plot.

On the other hand, it should be noted that the story ends with a nice pun. The last paragraph consists of two words with a comma between them and an exclamation point following: "Heigh" as in the Lone Ranger's cry of "Heigh ho, Silver," and the name of John Scott's horse—that is, "Heigh, *Danger!*"[2]

The third story, "Mind over Matter," appeared in *Blue Book* magazine a month after the second.[3] Nevins praises this story highly, putting it up with "Man Bites Dog" as one of Queen's eight best short fictions[4] and saying it has "a superb tight-knit plot with not a word wasted, and [it is] a joy to read even if you've never gone to a boxing match in your life."[5]

On the other hand, a less sympathetic reader may note that the mystery plot—the basic "givens" upon which Ellery's inductions are based—hinges on Ellery taking an old camel's-hair topcoat with him to a Heavyweight Championship fight on a warm night and then casually leaving it in the back seat of a roadster;[6] further, if the next car had not belonged to the champion's manager[7] or if the

---

[1] *Ibid.*

[2] *Ibid.*

[3] Nevins, p. 236.

[4] *Ibid.*, pp. 13–14.

[5] *Ibid.*, p. 68.

[6] *"New" Adventures*, p. 259.

[7] *Ibid.*, pp. 258–259.

killer had put on a shirt as well as a pair of pants,[1] the plot would not have worked; also, the plot depends on the new champion climbing out a window into an alley, walking down the alley, across a street, and into a parking lot soon after the championship fight--and not being recognized. And then he had to walk back.[2] Further, the former champion had to somehow get away from his manager and doctor soon after the fight in which he had taken a beating and make the same trip to his car--in his case, he *was* seen and recognized, but it was merely by his chauffeur, whom he had sent away.[3] Of course, Golden Age mysteries--those written between the World Wars--tend to have very artificial plots, but this one seems too artificial for its own good.

Perhaps it is the contrast to the boxing match which emphasizes this artificiality. Evidence can be found in these passages:

> When the gong clamored for the start of the third round, the champion's left eye was a purple slit, his lips were cracked and bloody, and his simian chest rose and fell in gasps.
>
> Thirty seconds later he was cornered, a beaten animal, above their heads [that is, Paula's and Ellery's, who are in the reporter's box]. They could see the ragged splotches over his kidneys, blooming above his trunks like crimson flowers.
>
> * * *
>
> At the count of nine, with the bay of the crowd in his flattened ears, Mike Brown staggered to his feet. The bulk of Coyle slipped in, shadowy, and pumped twelve solid, lethal gloves into Brown's body. The champion's knees broke. A whistling six-inch uppercut to the point of the jaw sent him toppling to the canvas.[4]

Other passages with their share of realism tied to the

---

[1] *Ibid.*, p. 280.

[2] *Ibid.*, pp. 280-281.

[3] *Ibid.*, p. 269.

[4] *Ibid.*, pp. 262-263.

sports world appear in the story, such as the description
of the victor's packed dressing room after the fight.[1]
The means of throwing the fight seems somewhat artificial, however—the champion fights without throwing
punches with his more powerful right hand. Perhaps it
is merely a comment on the present, visually-recorded
age, but that seems too easily checked.[2] A sports reporter, Phil Maguire, notices it in the story,[2] and even in 1939
some major fights were filmed.

What is especially interesting is that this is a thematic
fiction. The title, "Mind over Matter," shows the traditional conflict between intellect and brawn. Is this a
valid distinction? Probably not. The present writer
remembers when he was a graduate assistant in English
at the University of Oklahoma in the era of Bud Wilkin-
son; he never had a football player make less than a *C* in
freshman English.; baseball players and wrestlers were a
different matter. The point is the obvious one: that
intelligence is spread out among athletes. (There is also
a point about the types of athletes recruited, but that is
not significant here.)

Valid or not, this story is based upon this traditional
contrast. It is the contrast between Ellery and Jim Coyle,
the challenger—that is, between brains and brawn. It is
set up, in the traditional popular-fiction way, as a com-
petition between the two men for one woman—in this case,
Paula Paris. Here is how Coyle is introduced:

> The challenger appeared first....
> Miss Paris gasped with admiration. "Isn't he the
> one?"
> Jim Coyle was the one—an almost handsome
> giant six feet and a half tall, with preposterously
> broad shoulders, long smooth muscles, and a bronze
> skin....
> * * *
> "Hercules in trunks," breathed Miss Paris. "Did
> you ever see such a body, Ellery?"
> "The question more properly is," said Mr. Queen
> jealously, "can he keep that body off the floor?

---

[1] *Ibid.*, p. 264.

[2] *Ibid.*, p. 236.

That's the question, my girl."[1]

This by-play is continued in the dressing room. Coyle is introduced to Paula and immediately calls for the photographers to clear out, for he wants privacy—that is, privacy with Paula.[2] At one point, he says, "This lady and I got some sparring to do."[3] Their sparring before this was bantam-weight verbal, so to speak. When Phil Maguire, the reporter, shows up, Coyle asks him, "Say, this doll your mamie? If she ain't, I'm staking out my claim."[4] Moments later, this dialogue:

> "You're not going to stay in here while he dresses?" said Mr. Queen petulantly to Miss Paris. "Come on—you can wait for your hero in the hall."
> "Yes, sir," said Miss Paris submissively.
> Coyle guffawed. "Don't worry, fella. I ain't going to do you out of nothing. There's plenty of broads."

Despite the unusual submissiveness of a Hollywood columnist—Paula is in love with Ellery in these stories—the basic point is the humiliation of Ellery: how can brain compete with brawn? This is reinforced briefly afterward when Ellery walks Paula down the alley. He looks "through the shower-room window into the dressing room" where Coyle, Maguire, and Ellery's father are having a drink; echoing the thoughts of Ellery, the text says:

> Coyle in his athletic underwear was—well ...
> Mr. Queen hurried Miss Paris out of the alley and across the street to the parking lot.[5]

This conflict between intelligence and physicality is re-

---

[1] *Ibid.*, p. 261.

[2] *Ibid.*, pp. 264–265.

[3] *Ibid.*, p. 265.

[4] *Ibid.*

[5] *Ibid.*, p. 266.

solved when Ellery intellectually proves that Coyle has
killed Mike Brown, the former champion; the story ends
with these sentences:

> "Grab him, will you? My right isn't very good,"
> said Mr. Queen, employing a dainty and beautiful
> bit of footwork to escape Coyle's sudden homicidal
> lunge in his direction.
>
> And while Coyle went down under an avalanche
> of flailing arms and legs, Mr. Queen murmured
> apologetically to Miss Paris: "After all, darling, he
> *is* the heavyweight champion of the world."[1]

Implicit in this passage is the same division between
intellect and strength. Ellery avoids a physical attack;
and, while apologetic to Paula, nevertheless he has won:
Coyle is taken down by others due to what Ellery has
said.

This is an obvious example of popular fiction reinforcing popular attitudes, reinforcing a popular dichotomy.
But, unlike some fiction which would contrast the heroic
sportsman with the wimp, this is detective fiction: the
erudite detective, in the Sherlock Holmes' rationalistic
tradition, has always been a symbol of reason. The boxer
obviously has no chance against the inductive detective.
Perhaps the reason Nevins praises this story so highly is
not so much the plot as this rationalistic subtext.

But this contrast between brain and brawn is not *just*
a popular literature convention. Dannay seems to have
felt it strongly while growing up. In *The Golden Summer*,
"Danny" runs into various problems which he talks his
way out of--or fails to: he returns the admission price to
his "House of Horrors" to one boy who grabbed his neck
in an upset over a fake ghost ("as always, at the im-
mediate threat of physical violence, Danny quickly
surrendered"),[2] but he talks the threatening boys who
earlier paid for admission into holding off their demand
for the return of their money--twice;[3] he talks a dissatis-
fied lottery winner out of violence, by returning his--

---

[1] *Ibid.*, p. 281.

[2] *The Golden Summer*, p. 20.

[3] *Ibid.*, pp. 24-25, 32.

only his—cost of a ticket while letting him keep the prize book;[1] once, fearing the destruction of his club house, not fearing personal harm this time, Danny talks his peers into settling a financial disagreement by a trial;[2] another time, upset over being dismissed as a driver of a play wagon-train and unable to talk around the usurper, Danny fights—and loses[3]; under the threat of violence, he and his two closest friends let two bullies into their club;[4] and, finally, Danny sees a bigger boy with money the boy had stolen from him—but is unable to do anything about it.[5] The passage in the latter deserves quotation: "[Danny] trudged homeward, hating his puny body and his puny heart. He hated everything about himself—his weak eyes, his weak muscles, his weak will."[6] If this passage is autobiographical, as the book is, at least in general, then there is no surprise to the motif of "Mind over Matter." Danny Nathan in *The Golden Summer* was not able to get his money back—"If only he could devise some plan—some startling coup—that would pluck victory out of the burr patch of defeat!... Whenever a spark lit in his fevered brain, it was promptly snuffed out by that dark, terrifying shadow of Owgoost and his big, brawny fists"[7]—but Ellery Queen could avoid those fists and prove that intelligence was more significant than physical strength.

The last of these four stories is "Trojan Horse," published in *Blue Book* magazine in December of 1939, two months after "Mind over Matter."[8] It is a less complex story than "Mind over Matter" also. The basic plot turns

---

[1] *Ibid.*, pp. 75–77.

[2] *Ibid.*, p. 95.

[3] *Ibid.*, pp. 160–163.

[4] *Ibid.*, pp. 166–167.

[5] *Ibid.*, pp. 180–181.

[6] *Ibid.*, p. 181.

[7] *Ibid.*

[8] Nevins, p. 236.

on stolen jewels—a middle-aged fan of the Southern California Trojans buys for his daughter, who is engaged to the Southern California fullback, a hundred thousand dollars' worth of eleven matched sapphires.[1] During a pep talk "Pop" Wing, the legendary fan, gives the Trojans just before their Rose Bowl Game with the Carolina Spartans, in the Trojan dressing room, the jewels are stolen from his coat.

It must be said that, as a sports story, this work is disappointing. There is a running motif of the advice the fan has given his son-in-law-to-be about defeating Carolina.[2] This is the way it ends:

> Fourth down, seconds to go, and the ball on Carolina's 24-yard line! [The score is Carolina 6, USC 3.[3]]
> "If they don't go over next play," screamed Pop, "the game's lost. It'll be Carolina's ball and they'll freeze it.... *Roddy!*" he thundered. *"The kick play!"* [Roddy Crockett is the future son-in-law.]
> And, as if Roddy could hear that despairing voice, the ball snapped back, the Trojan quarterback snatched it, held it ready for Roddy's toe, his right hand between the ball and the turf.... Roddy darted up as if to kick, but as he reached the ball he scooped it from his quarterback's hands and raced for the Carolina goal line.
> * * *
> USC spread out, blocking like demons. The Carolina team was caught completely by surprise. Roddy wove and slithered through the bewildered Spartan line and crossed the goal just as the final whistle blew.[4]

Maybe in 1939, almost fifty years ago as this essay is written, that was an exciting trick play, rather than, as today, one of the standard trick plays (except that,

---

[1] *"New" Adventures,* pp. 291, 293.

[2] *Ibid.,* pp. 287-288, 294, 303, 304.

[3] *Ibid.,* pp. 300, 303.

[4] *Ibid.,* p. 304.

today, the holder is the one who runs or passes)—one which is normally guarded against. At any rate, the material has not worn well: the surprise is too familiar. One can read it with historical appreciation primarily.

It is notable that a number of other details are also historical. For example, when "Pop" Wing and his group enter the Trojan dressing room, Roddy Crockett is "lacing his doeskin pants."[1] In his speech to the team, "Pop" Wing mentions USC's Rose Bowl victories in 1923, 1930, 1932, and 1933.[2] It is also notable that Roddy Crockett and his nemesis on the Carolina side, Ostermoor, play both offense and defense—for example, Crockett encourages "one of his linesmen" while Carolina has the ball;[3] indeed, two or so plays later, Ostermoor throws a pass for a touchdown.[4] Ostermoor is also praised for his highly accurate kicking.[5] A bit later Crockett carries the ball for a 44-yard gain, but the Trojans do not make a touchdown, for Ostermoor breaks up two plays; then Crockett kicks a field goal.[6] All of these references are from the first half of the game; however, they show that Crockett and Ostermoor not only play both ways, Ostermoor's passing balancing Crockett's running on offense, but they also are the kickers. Even in the 1930s, this sounds like a stylistic simplification, to avoid confusing the reader with a number of team members' names.

There are other details which seem distinctly odd but which are due to changes since the time of the story. For example, the football for the game is uninflated in the dressing room of the host team shortly before the game,[7]

---

[1] *Ibid.*, p. 295.

[2] *Ibid.*, p. 296.

[3] *Ibid.*, p. 298.

[4] *Ibid.*

[5] *Ibid.*, p. 299.

[6] *Ibid.*, p. 300.

[7] *Ibid.*, p. 306.

and there is only one ball used in the entire game.[1]

Despite some of these historical oddities, one of the touches in the story is nicely done, as true now as it was then:

> New Year's Day was warm and sunny; and Mr. Queen felt strange as he prepared to pick up Paula Paris and escort here to the Wing estate, from which their party was to proceed to the Pasadena stadium. In his quaint Eastern fashion, he was accustomed to don a mountain of sweater, scarf, and overcoat when he went to a football game; and here he was *en route* in a sports jacket!
>
> "California, thy name is Iconoclast," muttered Mr. Queen....[2]

Also, the opening of the game is nicely described, despite the cliché of a groan rending the skies:

> Kick-off! Twenty-two figures race to converge in a tumbling mass, and the stands thundered, the USC section fluttered madly with flags ... and then there was a groan that rent the blue skies, and deadly, despairing silence.
>
> For the Trojans' safety man caught the ball, started forward, slipped, the ball popped from his hands, the Carolina right end fell on it––and there was the jumping, gleeful Spartan team on the Tro-jan's 9-yard line, Carolina's ball, first down, and four plays for a touchdown.[3]

Fumbled kick returns are a familiar part of football; and, since no one is claiming that this is a clever new trick play––just a common difficulty in the art of football––its appearance here is quite acceptable.

Besides the sports details,a the most interesting aspect of the story is the classical allusions. In the thorough development of this motif, this work is typical of many later Queen novels which set up metaphoric or

---

[1] *Ibid.*, pp. 305–306.

[2] *Ibid.*, p. 291.

[3] *Ibid.*, p. 297, ellipsis in the original.

symbolic patterns which run through the work (such as the Darwinian pattern and animal imagery of *The Origin of Evil* [1951]). The most obvious suggestion is that of the gridiron war between the Spartans and the Trojans, since the Trojan War in the *Iliad* arose from a grievance between Menelaos, King of Sparta, and Paris, Price of Troy.

The University of Southern California team, of course, was then, as now, the Trojans. But where did Queen get his Spartans? In the story, they are just said to be from "Carolina," with no indication of North or South (286 et seq.). Doyle Boggs, the Director of Communications at Wofford College, Spartanburg, South Carolina, wrote the present author this comment:

> I am afraid I am not going to be much help to you. Wofford College's athletic teams have been the "Terriers" for at least 75 years, apparently taking their name from a real dog that once served as a baseball mascot. The college colors, Old Gold and Black, also seems natural for a Boston Terrier. The local high school sometimes has used the nickname "Spartans," but its teams officially have been known by various other names, including "Vikings," "Crimson Tide" and "Red Birds" over the years.
>
> I am fairly certain that no football playing colleges in the Carolinas are known as the Spartans, although we do have Lions vs. Christians (Mars Hill vs. Elon) every year. I guess the author [Ellery Queen] must have been thinking of Michigan State.[1]

Since Boggs writes of the present time for the two states, it is still barely possible that in 1939 there was a Spartan team from one of the Carolinas; but probably, as the lack of a North or South identification suggests, the team was invented for Queen's purpose. (Perhaps commercial considerations—of not upsetting any supporters of actual teams—were involved in inventing the losing side.)

Paula Paris denies that there is a Helen to this "war," but she identifies "Pop" Wing as Priam, King of Troy, calling him in a parody of Shakespeare, "the noblest

---

[1] Doyle Boggs, personal letter to the author, 4 April 1988.

Trojan of them all."[1] When Roddy Crockett leaves the
Wing household for the game, he is described as "the
pride of Troy [who] went loping off to the wars, leaping
into his roadster and waving farewell...."[2] At the climax
of the case, Ellery recites what he calls "a parable,"
which is the story of the Trojan Horse[3]—in short, the
story shifts the classical parallels from the football game
to the missing-jewels puzzle. The solution to the mystery
seems to this writer unlikely, but it is not as absurd as
the plot of "Mind over Matter"—that is, it is acceptable
as a Golden Age puzzle; however, frustrating Queen's
fame as a fair-play puzzle writer, one necessary fact,
based on football practices of the time but no longer
true, is omitted before the solution mentions it—Queen
was counting on the 1930's common knowledge.

As indicated, the plot involves an unintended parallel
to the Trojan Horse, for which both the story's title and
the parable prepared the reader—unintended by the
criminal, that is. The development of this series of
classical parallels is typical, as has been said, of one of
the distinctive aspects of Queen's better later writings:
Dannay, the plotter and motif-builder of the cousins, was
beginning to sharpen his skills in this story. Perhaps
this classical motif is not completely significant for this
paper on the use of sports; but, as was indicated, at first
it is used to reinforce the football "warfare"—with the
Trojans winning (for once!) the Trojan War.

What may be said of these four stories? First, two of
them are historically important within popular literature,
as Queen himself commented in the notes to *Sporting
Blood:* "Man Bits Dog", was the first baseball-mystery
short story published,[4] and "Trojan Horse", was the first
football-mystery short story published,[5] although an
author named Cortland Fitzsimmons had written about

---

[1] *"New" Adventures,* p. 286, repeated authorially at
p. 294.

[2] *Ibid.,* p. 294.

[3] *Ibid.,* p. 305.

[4] *Sporting Blood,* p. 59.

[5] *Ibid.,* p. 119.

those sports in mystery *novels* earlier.[1]

Second, they are, in several different ways, interesting examples of the content of popular literature: in the use of a woman's ignorance of baseball as an expository device; in the use of conventional characters in conventional plots (here illustrated only in "Long Shot"); more significantly, in the reinforcing of the popular beliefs about the contrast between mind and body. Some readers may object to these conventional aspects being called "interesting," but, for a student, they are revealing. In all popular literature, there is a tension between the conventional and the new—with the basic intention of producing a fresh conventionality. And material may be interesting to a student which is irritating to a different type of reader.

Third, these stories are also interesting as popular *art,* for popular literature may also have certain types of aesthetic delights. One of those here is in the mythic motifs in the last story, even if the Trojan War is invoked more as a pleasant (perhaps thrilling) game than as something more meaningful; but another aesthetic delight, one with great significance, lies in the capturing of American life at a certain period—in this paper, the details of sports have been emphasized. Anthony Boucher was right when he said that mysteries, among having other virtues, were Hamlet's "abstracts and brief chronicles of the time";[2] and sports—professional baseball, horseracing, professional boxing, and collegiate football—are part of the American times.

Acknowledgements

A shortened version of this paper was read at the 1987 annual Meeting of the Sports Literature Association, 30 September, in Fort Worth, Texas. In the program the paper was called "Sports as Background in Popular Literature," but that was a whim of one of the persons in charge of the meeting. The author had used that phrase,

---

[1] *Ibid.*

[2] Francis M. Nevins, Jr., and Martin H. Greenberg, eds. *Exeunt Murderers: The Best Mystery Stories of Anthony Boucher.* Carbondale, Illinois: Southern Illinois University Press (Mystery Makers Series), 1983, p. xv.

without capitals and not in quotation marks, in his cover letter with the submission; the program preparer must have thought it sounded more academic than the actual title. The author thanks Francis M. Nevins, Jr., who came to his rescue with a Xerox of "Man Bites Dog" when he wanted to check the baseball players' names in the paperback he was consulting at that time against the original book's text. (The Hollywood references in one of the other stories had been updated, but the baseball references were not changed.) Nevins also suggested one of the parallels to *The Golden Summer.* At the meeting, the preceding speaker, Eric Solomon of San Francisco State University, speaking of Jews in baseball-detective stories and novels, pointed out the significance of the boy in "Man Bites Dog," although he did not realize that "Ellery Queen" was Jewish. One of the people in the back of the room, in the discussion after the paper, drew the author's attention to Spartanburg, South Carolina; and Doyle Boggs, Director of Communications, Wofford College, in Spartanburg, kindly replied to this author's letter, as was quoted in the paper. Finally, the author thanks Ron Newsome of the Department of Health and Physical Education, Tarleton State University, who confirmed some of the historic football details in "Trojan Horse."

WORKS CITED

Boggs, Doyle. Personal letter to the author, 4 April 1988.

Nevins, Francis M., Jr. *Royal Bloodline: Ellery Queen, Author and Detective.* Bowling Green, Ohio: Bowling Green University Popular Press, 1974.

_____, and Martin H. Greenberg, eds. *Exeunt Murderers: The Best Mystery Stories of Anthony Boucher.* Carbondale: Southern Illinois University Press (Mystery Makers series), 1983.

_____, and Ray Stanich. *The Sound of Detection: Ellery Queen's Adventures in Radio.* Madison, Indiana: Brownstone Books, 1983.

Queen, Ellery. *The "New" Adventures of Ellery Queen, Including an Amazing Short Novel "The Lamp of God."* New York: Frederick A. Stokes, 1940.

_____, ed. *Sporting Blood: The Great Sports Detective Stories.* Boston: Little, Brown, 19421. (The edition checked was that of Blue Ribbon Books [Garden City, New York, 1946], a hardcover reprint which changed the title to the subtitle but used the original plates.)

The Gold Medal Boys
George Tuttle

The lead article in the October 1951 issue of the *Writer's Digest* loudly proclaimed: "Gold Medal Now Buying 7 Books a Month—$2,000 minimum guarantee." This was big news to mystery writers since the average hardcover novelist was earning only $2,500 a year,[1] and the pulps, which didn't pay any better, were dying out.

Gold Medal was a new market of incredible opportunity. It changed the nature of the publishing industry to the advantage of the writer. First, because it paid royalties based on the number of copies printed. (All other publishers paid on the number of copies sold. With Gold Medal, the writer got all of his money up front.) Second, it guaranteed a minimum advance of $2,000. (Some major hardcover publishers had been known not to pay an advance.[2] For a mystery writer of the 1950's, $2,000 was a fantastic sum.) Third, it was not unusual for a Gold Medal book to sell a million copies or more. (This was a fact that was good for both the ego and the pocketbook.) Fourth, Gold Medal was a large market for detective fiction, particularly hardboiled detective fiction. (This was good in the light of the dying pulp market.) And finally, Gold Medal didn't ask writers to sign away subsidiary rights. (Hardcover publishers usually asked

---

[1] The $2,500 figure comes from an article by Bill Lengel called "Bill Lengel Says It Again" *(Writer's Digest,* 34 [Sept. 1954], p. 74-78).

[2] Dutton, for one, did not pay advances on some of the mysteries it published.

for 50 percent of the money paid for the paperback rights, plus a share of movie and other subsidiary rights.)

Gold Medal was the brainchild of Fawcett Publications, publisher of *True, Mechanix Illustrated,* and other popular magazines. Prior to starting the Gold Medal line in 1949, Fawcett's experience with paperbacks had been as the distributor for Signet, the company that released multi-million sellers *I, the Jury* and *God's Little Acre.* Given its success as a distributor, Fawcett saw no reason why it would not be able to do for itself what it had done for Signet, but there was one roadblock in the way of starting a paperback line.   Fawcett's contract with Signet stated that Fawcett could not publish a competitive line of reprint paperbacks.   The contract said nothing about original, non-reprint paperbacks, however, and crafty Fawcett took advantage of this omission.

Gold Medal was created in the belief that there were many people who wanted to read good original fiction and non-fiction, but who didn't want to pay hardcover prices. The people at Fawcett believed that they had, through their experience, the ability to market a line of 25-cent paperback originals, a line of Westerns, adventure yarns, true-crime stories, and suspense novels that were not reprints but original works.

The key to Gold Medal's success was attracting talented writers, writers who would make the Gold Medal emblem a seal of quality.   To attract these writers, GM offered large advances and let its money do the talking.

Cornell Woolrich, Sax Rohmer, W.T. Ballard, Lester Dent, Octavus Roy Cohen, Steve Fisher, Brett Halliday (who co-wrote a couple of books under the name of Matthew Blood), and W.R. Burnett are examples of the veteran talent Gold Medal attracted. These authors were no doubt impressed by the big money Fawcett had to offer, money that often exceeded the amounts hardcover publishers were willing to pay.   But besides attracting proven writers, GM also developed a large amount of young talent. Gold Medal discovered writers like Richard Prather, Charles Williams, Peter Rabe, John McPartland, Gil Brewer, Richard Himmell, Ovid Demaris, Marvin Albert (a.k.a. Albert Conroy and Nick Quarry), Lionel White, and Vin Packer.   John D. MacDonald also published his first book and many to follow under the Gold Medal insignia. Other young authors like Bruno Fischer, Wade Miller, Edward Aarons, David Goodis, Day Keene, Harry Whittington, Jonathan Craig, and Stephen Marlowe started with other publishers but became Gold Medal regulars. This young talent was especially important to Gold Medal's success. GM seemed to thrive on young writers who could offer a fresh point of view, a point of view that wasn't a slave to action, and who understood the importance of character development. This young talent, in particular, brought in the readers and established Gold Medal as a publisher of million sellers.

According to Alice Hackett's book *70 Years of Best Sellers*, there were fifty-six mysteries released during the 1950's that sold a million or more copies. Of the fifty-six, nineteen were written by Erle Stanley Gardner, seven by Ian Fleming, and six by Mickey Spillane. Of the remaining twenty-four, twenty-three were published by Gold Medal.[1] These twenty-three books were written by eight authors. Richard Prather led the pack with fourteen titles, John D. MacDonald had three, and Bruno Fischer, Charles Williams, Gil Brewer, Richard Himmell, David Goodis, and Lee Roberts each had one. During the 1950's, no other paperback-original publisher came near GM's success. Singlehandedly, Gold Medal made the paperback original an important medium for crime fiction and, by doing so, cut into the sales of hardcover mysteries. In 1953, Anthony Boucher reported a twenty-five percent drop in the number of hardcover books sent to him to review. He attributed this drop to "the phenomenal growth of original paperback publishing."[2]

William Lengel and Ralph Daigh worked together with the Fawcett family to manage Gold Medal. Jim Bishop was their first editor, but he left after only a few titles to pursue a very fruitful freelance writing career. In his place, Lengel selected a former Hollywood scriptwriter named Richard Carroll.

Carroll was the man who ensured the standard of high quality that sustained GM throughout the fifties and long after, when other editors had taken over. Though it is

---

[1] Gold Medal also had some million-selling non-mysteries like Theodore Pratt's *The Tormented,* Vin Packer's *Spring Fire* and Tereska Torres' *Women's Barracks.*

[2] Quote from Boucher's "Criminals at Large," *New York Times Book Review,* 29 March 1953, p. 26.

true that much of the line's success was due to Fawcett's ability to market its product, Gold Medal would never have earned its top position in the publishing field if it hadn't had a man like Carroll to guarantee the product's quality. Dell and Popular Library produced fabulous covers and understood newsstand distribution quite well, but Gold Medal still topped them in sales, and Richard Carroll was one reason why.

Through suggesting ideas and requests for rewrites, Carroll helped good writers reach their ultimate potential. He had the ability to make a million-selling author out of an unknown. Literary agent Donald MacCampbell in his book, *Don't Step on It—It Might Be a Writer,* dedicated a whole chapter to this editor. In this chapter, MacCampbell states, "He (Carroll) had a faculty for creating writers out of mailmen, bank clerks, Western Union operators, even bartenders—I think he could have trained a Neanderthal to write books for him." MacCampbell also writes, "Editors are plentiful in New York. But there was only one Carroll and I doubt if we shall ever again see his equal."

But still, to some people, Carroll's job must have seemed easy. Fawcett had an ability to attract good writers. So all the editor had to do was have them add a little sex in the tradition of Mickey Spillane or Erskine Caldwell and the public would buy it. For during the fifties it was obvious that sex sold. You could see it on every paperback cover—full-figured women and bountiful bust lines were common. But editor Carroll knew it wasn't that simple and had no patience with writers who just threw in sex. He once criticized a writer by saying, "If he shakes his goddamn book, the sex scenes will all fall out." Carroll realized that if sex was going to enhance a story, it had to be an essential part of the plot, not an indiscriminate or haphazard act. He stated, "I want sex to be glued to the action, not just dragged in to titillate."[1] And for Gold Medal sex was often the essential ingredient to the story, so essential that Gold Medal novels often were centered more around relationships, both sexual and emotion than around crime and violence. These relationships brought an extra dimension to Gold Medal fiction, a dimension that was not present in

---

[1] Quotes from *Don't Step on It—It Might Be a Writer.*

the old pulp magazines.

But Gold Medal's success was based on more than its ability to use sex. Carroll recognized that the key to good fiction is creativity, and he did not want Gold Medal fiction to be confined to only the old traditions of the hardboiled detective story. Though GM produced its share of private-detective thrillers (Richard Prather's Shell Scott is still one of the most successful private-eye series ever), it relied more heavily on non-series fiction and heroes from different walks of life. In Bruno Fischer's *Fools Walk In* (1951) the protagonist is a high-school English teacher, in Charles Williams' *A Touch of Death* (1954) he is a 25-year-old former football star, and in Wade Miller's *Kitten with a Whip* (1959) he's an engineer at an aircraft plant. GM liked using everyday people as heroes, characters that the public cold identify with, heroes who found themselves drawn out of their regular world and into an unfamiliar, exciting world of violence, lust, and fear.

GM also had no reservations about using antiheroes. As Carroll would say, "There's nothing wrong with an antihero. The world is full of them."[1] So in Peter Rabe's *A House in Naples* (1956) the story is built around a G.I. deserter who is working Italy's black market, and in John McPartland's *The Kingdom of Johnny Cool* (1959) the plot is centered around a Sicilian bandit turned hitman who tries a single-handed takeover of the underworld. In both cases, the writer made a reprehensible protagonist interesting and sympathetic to the reader and proved that one didn't need a virtuous good guy to have a popular book.

Nor had GM any reservations about publishing novels that didn't have a protagonist. Books like John D. Mac-Donald's *The Damned* (1952), Wade Miller's *South of the Sun* (1953), or Vin Packer's *The Girl on the Best Seller List* (1960) relied on an ensemble case of characters, each character having his or her own story, with plot lines converging to create a single tale. Novels without protagonists are an example of Gold Medal's willingness to experiment.

Another example of this willingness can be found with the Gold Medal giants, 35-cent super-novels that stretched the traditional 60,000-word format usually

---

[1] *Ibid.*

associated with detective fiction. Novels like Richard
Gehman's *Driven,* H. Vernor Dixon's *To Hell Together,* or
Richard Prather and Stephen Marlowe's *Double in Trouble*
were twice the length of the average suspense thriller
and offered the reader a meatier alternative to the typical
quick read.

Gold Medal was also one of the first publishers to
introduce the backwoods into hardboiled fiction. Its first
backwoods thriller, Charles Williams' *Hill Girl,* sold over a
million and led the way for books like *Mountain Girl*
(1953) by Cord Wainer (Thomas B. Dewey), *Hell's Our
Destination* (1953) by Gil Brewer, and *Desire in the Dust*
(1956) by Harry Whittington. Williams and Whittington
were particularly skilled at this brand of fiction. They
were able to use the backwoods setting time and again to
create a primitive backdrop to the passion and violence
of life. This setting was a refreshing break from the
traditional urban settings and characters of hardboiled
fiction.

Spy fiction was another variation in the traditional
hardboiled formula. Gold Medal's foray into the world of
espionage began in 1950, with its first fiction release,
John Flagg's *The Persian Cat.* Besides Flagg, who wrote
a number of noteworthy spy novels, E. Howard Hunt was
another early contributor with books like *The Violent
Ones* (1950) and *I Came To Kill* (1953, written under the
name Gordon Davis, and Richard Himmel with efforts like
The Chinese Keyhole (1951). In 1955 GM initiated two
popular espionage series, Edward S. Aaron's Sam Durell
and Stephen Marlowe's Chester Drum. Spy fiction was a
successful alternative to the private-eye yarn (though
in the case of Chester Drum, the reader had the best of
both worlds). It provided readers with exotic settings
and catered to the interest of a post-World War II public
more concerned about world affairs. And with the
escalation of the Cold War, more spy series popped up.
In 1960, Donald Hamilton's Matt Helm debuted in *Death of
a Citizen.* Philip Atlee followed in 1963, with his Joe Gall
series, and in 1969 Dan J. Marlowe reintroduced a character he had created back in 1962—Earl Drake—and started
a series that won him an Edgar. Gold Medal has provided
readers with a wealth of spy fiction. Because of the
quality and quantity of these works, Fawcett has been
one of the most significant contributors to the concept of
American espionage fiction.

Fawcett Gold Medal had a huge impact on detective

fiction in general and the hardboiled school in particular. It established the paperback original as a major medium for detective fiction, selling millions of copies. It developed a large amount of young talent (Prather, Williams, Rabe, etc.). It generated a number of popular series (Travis McGee, Sam Durell, Matt Helm, etc.), as well as a wealth of non-series fiction. It gave writers a fertile environment in which to be creative (Octavus Roy Cohen compared writing for Gold Medal to writing with "his gloves off"). And finally, it rejuvenated the hardboiled school, giving this style of writing a much needed shot in the arm. During the 1940's, hardboiled fiction, with the exception of a few noteworthy talents, had become stale. There was no longer a creative force like the *Black Mask* of Capt. Joe Shaw's days. With the advent of Gold Medal, hardboiled fiction boomed with new life.

Gold Medal always kept its high standards. When Richard Carroll died in the late 1950's, he was replaced with Knox Burger, editor from chief rival Dell. As a result, while other publishers of paperback originals died out, Gold Medal survived and remained successful. Today, Gold Medal originals from the fifties and sixties are still being reprinted and praised.

Additional Bibliography

Daigh, Ralph. *Maybe You Should Write a Book.* Englewood
    Cliffs, NJ: Prentice-Hall, 1977
"Gold Medal Now Buying 7 Books a Month--$2,000 Minimum
    Guarantee." *Writer's Digest,* 31 (Oct. 1951), p. 15-20,
    73-75.
MacCampbell, Donald. *Don't Step on It--It Might Be a
    Writer.* Los Angeles: Sherbourne Press, 1972.
Sugg, Redding S., Jr. "Introduction." *Cabin Road,* by
    John Faulkner, p. vii-xxv.
White, Jon. "Knox Burger: An Interview." *Paperback
    Forum,* (issue #2, 1985), p. 4-10.

Further Gems from the Literature
William F. Deeck

Providence continues to work in mysterious ways:
   A high-pitched voice he had, as if by some special dispensation of providence he had eunuch blood in him.--*The Case of the Platinum Blonde*, by Christopher Bush

Whom do you believe?
   How do you overcome the psychic blow when you see that an editor has changed your title *Suitable for Framing* to *Kickback for a Killer?*--Hank Searls, introduction to *The Adventures of Mike Blair*
   "A Dish of Homicide" (originally titled "Suitable for Framing") was published in *Dime Detective* for November 1949.--Robert Weinberg, afterword to *The Adventures of Mike Blair*

The verbed-noun horror strikes again:
   It had to be the specter of the long-dead Cavalier Sir Byng Rawdon who ghosted into the Oak Room at Telford Old Hall one night....--Back cover, Zebra edition of Carter Dickson's *The Cavalier's Cup*

   "Tildy's been having us private-eyed?"--*Price Tag for Murder*, by Spencer Dean

   "Well, well--daisies, too!" baritoned the sculptor.--*Experiment Perilous*, by Margaret Carpenter

   "Do you call that female intuition?" he wise-assed.--*Lamaar Ransom--Private Eye*, by David Galloway

Metaphor run riot:

A very down-to-earth killer was on the loose, and it was up to Sir Henry to bring the footpad to heel and take him in tow before he had time to make tracks for his next victim!--Back cover blurb for Zebra edition of *She Died a Lady*, by Carter Dickson

The moment had come, as in every case, to cut through intangibles, get down to bedrock and talk turkey.--*Death Demands an Audience*, by Helen Reilly

Serious advice from the Famous Detective:
"... You must fire without hesitation--but do not shoot a member of Scotland Yard!"--*The Merrivale Mystery*, by James Corbett

The Famous Detective is more than a brain:
Moreton scaled the wall without difficulty, but Bancroft, more bulky, was glad when the feat was accomplished. Serge went over the obstacle at a bound....--*The Merrivale Mystery*, by James Corbett

Come now, Sir Henry, rethink this:
... The famous detective Sir Henry Merrivale didn't believe in a gunman who could walk through the air.--Back cover blurb for Zebra edition of *She Died a Lady*, by Carter Dickson

How's-that-again? department:
His black eyes held a protuberant glitter, as though constantly groping for attention to the crooked smile below.--*The Man with Bated Breath*, by Joseph B. Carr

"Don't you realise that those who have to spend an English winter in the country spend their time brooding over imaginary grievances, and if they have none they create them?"--*Murder by Burial*, by Stanley Casson

I had a few theories of my own, and I decided to let them jell before I put my foot into it.--*Death of an Ad Man*, by Alfred Eichler

The wind blew hard around the old house, tormenting it in every wrack and sinew.--*Death Demands an Audience*, by Helen Reilly
"The poison is unknown and nearly undetectable."--*Fellowship of Fear*, by Aaron J. Elkins

Murdock stopped, his smile smothered in the depths of his gaze.--*The Jade Venus,* by George Harmon Coxe

Were her words those of a demented woman who is going insane?--*The Merrivale Mystery,* by James Corbett

... His soul ached for the smell of hot water.--*The Door with Seven Locks,* by Edgar Wallace

There were lots of unexplored corners remaining in this sordid morass.--*Spider House,* by Van Wyck Mason

Marleen nodded, an expression of incredulous interest glazed on to her face.--*The Wooden Overcoat,* by Pamela Branch

She was helping to uncover further facts, facts that would add a last tremendous iota to the crushing weight....--*Death--by Appointment,* by James Corbett

The sixth instinct possessed by all good reporters persuaded him that there was something about this matter that did not show on the surface.--*For Sale--Murder,* by Will Levinrew

... The character he had so skillfully assumed seemed to synchronise with his surroundings.--*The Lion's Mouth,* by James Corbett

"She was sinking into an unconscious coma...."--*The Merrivale Mystery,* by James Corbett

Neatest tricks of the week:
As he shook hands, the newcomer exhaled an odour of Harris tweed and whiskey....--*Murder in Silence,* by George Selmark

She could see thoughts moving behind the pale-blue of his eyes.--*First Come, First Kill,* by Francis Allan

Then a deep flush swept up his throat, over his face, and into the roots of his blond hair.--*First Come, First Kill*, by Francis Allan

There was a thick film of dust on the water in the pan.--*Curtains for the Copper*, by Thomas Polsky

The hollowness in her stomach congealed into reality.--*First Come, First Kill*, by Francis Allan

We counted what we'd taken. There were twenty-five thousand-dollar bills, thirty-one five-hundred-dollar bills, twenty-seven two-hundred-dollar bills, and sixty-two one-hundred-dollar bills.--*The Fifth Grave*, by Jonathan Latimer

The sleek dames were something else again, in *senorita* outfits with cleavage to the belly button....--*Corpus Delectable*, by Talmage Powell

[He] Got up, switched on the light, then went and lay prone upon the bed again, staring at the ceiling through aching eyes.--*The Silent House*, by John G. Brandon

Her face was startled.--*Death Demands an Audience*, by Helen Reilly

"The man in back of the exit door got him from behind, pinned his arms to his sides before he could shoot, and knifed him at the same time."--*Death Knell*, by Baynard Kendrick

A very perceptive detective observes:
A compact woman in her early forties, her muscles were taut beneath the shorts she was wearing.--*Not Till a Hot January*, by M.J. Adamson

Marvelous medical precision in dealing with arsenic poisoning:
"She would have gone under in seven minutes, but I gave her a strong emetic which produced wonderful results, and she will be normal in fifteen minutes."--*The Merrivale Mystery*, by James Corbett

Ah, the good old days:
His idea was that a shirt with French cuffs could be worn two weeks instead of one.--*The Cat and the Clock*, by Charles G. Booth

Inspector McKee goes the palmists one better:
McKee was interested in hands. The butler's was soft, with a thick, insensitive palm, a predatory thumb and heavy fingers pointed at the tips. It expressed cunning, greed, sensuality and cowardice.--*Dead Man Control*, by Helen Reilly

A psychologist is interrupted during an original observation:
"There are lucky days, when you had better stay at home, and unlucky ones--"--*Enrollment Cancelled (Dead Babes in the Wood)*, by D.B. Olsen

Interesting and amusing, yes, but there seems to be a small catch; or the club with a death wish:
"I don't expect you know quite how it is done--as a matter of fact it is rather interesting and amusing. We have a large square box, in the front of which is a round aperture; the contraption looks rather like one of those cameras which face-photographers use, with an immense lens. Each voter is given two small black marbles and he inserts his hand, clutching both marbles, into the lens-aperture of the box. No one can see what he does when once his hand is inside. Actually there are three receptacles inside the box. One is for white marbles, on the left; one for black marbles, on the right; the third is for those who do not wish to vote either way. If you decide to vote for the candidate, you place the white marble in the left-hand section and the black into the third neutral box. If you wish to vote against the candidate, you put the black ball only in the right-hand section, and the white one you deposit in the neutral box. If you don't want to vote at all, yet don't want the other people to know that you are not voting, you deposit both marbles in the neutral box. When the box is opened after the voting is over the secretary counts up the number of white balls, and if they are enough, and there is no black marble in the right-hand section, the candidate is elected."

An Australian Bibliomystery: Ligny's Lake

Michael J. Tolley

In 1967 the Australian Prime Minister, Sir Harold Holt, went missing, believed drowned, near Portsea in Victoria. In 1971, Sidney Hobson Courtier had his eighteenth novel, *Ligny's Lake*. published in London by Robert Hale and in New York by Simon and Schuster. Lewis Ligny, a space-research engineer in Canberra, is reported missing, believed drowned, at Bateman's Bay in New South Wales, the favoured coastal resort for those who live in the nation's capital. The etymological links between the names of Holt and Ligny (and some other parallels) clearly establish a deliberate, teasing connection between the two, which at first is almost suggestive of a *roman a clef*. Several people wanted Ligny's death, but one who did not, who called him a friend though he did not know him well, is the story's narrator, Sandy Carmichael, also an engineer. Sandy happens to see Ligny at a boxing match in Melbourne, five hundred miles away from the place he was supposed drowned, and on the same day.

Sandy begins a quest for Ligny, despite being warned off and even physically attacked by security men. His principal clue is in a stolen book he finds in Ligny's study, an edition of Thoreau's *Walden* which happens to have an illustration of Walden Pond in it that is the same shape as a model lake (with fully-working trains and ships) in Ligny's home. The book itself was a school prize and so gives Sandy a starting point in his search. He visits the book's owner and embarks on a fascinating and dangerous manhunt, in a race against others who think Ligny murdered three men closely related to them.

It would spoil the reader's pleasure in a good thriller which is, I am sure, not very well known today, if I were to say much more about the ingenious plotting of *Ligny's Lake*. For those who have read the book, however, I can offer some intriguing notes (made in the course of a paper on some ideas of place, real and imagined, in literature). I may however add here that not only the illustration in Thoreau's book (which does not appear in all printings), but also the accompanying text, is significant in the unravelling of the mystery of Ligny's whereabouts. Ultimately, it turns out that Thoreau's pond has a meaning in the life of the man who modelled his own lake upon it that resonates with a significance deeper than that usually associated with "mere" plotting.

Ligny's Lake does not appear in the checklist of bibliomysteries so lovingly compiled by John and Emily Ballinger (see "Collecting Bibliomysteries," by John Ballinger, *The Armchair Detective*, vol. 18, no. 2 [Spring 1985], 127–139 [list continued into vol. 18, no. 3]). I am sure that when he discovers it, John Ballinger will wish to give Courtier's novel a relatively high place among a group of mysteries that includes some of the best of all those in the wider genre. Courtier himself, once ranked by Julian Symons among Australian writers with Upfield, and "a good deal more ingenious" (see E.F. Bleiler in John M. Reilly's *Twentieth-Century Crime and Mystery Writers*, New York: St. Martin's Press, 1980), is apparently overdue for extensive reprinting.

It's About Crime
Marvin Lachman

Awed by the reputation of its author and his Edgar-winning first novel, I have made three attempts to get through Ross Thomas's *The Cold War Swap* (1965). The third, and most recent, try, in a reprint from Perennial Library, $3.95, was not the charm, and I gave up at page seventy. This spy story, set on both sides of Germany's wall, shows patches of good writing but is basically contrived with cynical, uninteresting characters caught in the usual web of international treachery. Seemingly to pad the book, Thomas has his characters consume an incredible amount of alcohol. If it were possible to get cirrhosis from reading a book, I would now have liver disease. Instead, I merely acquired a case of acute boredom.

A good remedy for the above was to go back to a simpler time and reread *Keeper of the Keys* (1932), by Earl Derr Biggers, the last of the Charlie Chan novels, reprinted by Mysterious Press, $3.95. Those who know Chan only from the B movies of the '30s and '40s will be pleasantly surprised at how readable and well plotted the six books about him are. Charlie, at Lake Tahoe to find the missing son of millionaire Dudley Ward, encounters his first taste of snow. The plotting is deft, and there is depth in the portrayal of Chan, especially his reactions to bigotry and "Americanization." Aphorisms, those sayings which occur in most Chan movies, seem more appropriate here as they embody Chan's detective methods. As he gathers clues, he says, "We must collect in leisure what we may use in haste. The fool in a hurry drinks his tea with a fork." When Chan sits down to weigh the clues, he remarks, "Thought is a lady, beautiful as

jade.... Events of tonight make me certain I must not
neglect the lady's company longer." Most mysteries written more than fifty years ago are far more dated. Fortunately, the Chan series (all available from Mysterious
Press) are notable exceptions.

The best work on mysteries in the British village is
the chapter by Mary Jean De Marr in *Comic Crime* (1987),
edited by Earl Bargainnier and published by Bowling
Green's Popular Press. Although Ms. De Marr covered
some recent examples, I suspect that she hadn't caught
up with John Greenwood's series (also of six book) about
Inspector John Mosley, whose territory covers the small
towns on the very flexible border between the counties
of York and Lancaster. British-village mysteries, contrasted with the generally unsophisticated examples of
rural-American detective stories, are told in a sophis-
ticated style and permit the reader to have fun at the
expense of the local characters. Greenwood, the pseudonym of the late John Buxton Hilton, was excellent on atmosphere, if a bit weak on plotting. Prime examples are
the third and fourth books in the series, *Mosley by
Moonlight* (1985; reprinted by Bantam, $2.95) in which a
British television crew invades the town of Hadley Dale
when extraterrestrial sightings are reported and *Mists
over Mosley* (1986), published in the U.S. by Walker,
$15.95, about a coven of witches and municipal corrup-
tion. Mosley is an unusually enigmatic sleuth, one who
likes to "keep himself to himself" as the British say. He
has a knack of disappearing but then turning up under
strange circumstances, properly surprising Greenwood
readers.

I'm especially fond of regional mysteries, especially
those set in New Mexico, a state as beautiful as any in
the United States. Fortunately, the state has had some
good mystery writers use it, including Richard Martin
Stern, Tony Hillerman, and Dorothy B. Hughes in *Ride the
Pink Horse* (1946), reprinted by Carroll and Graf, $3.95.
Many mystery fans remember the excellent movie based
on it and, indeed, the cover of this reprint portrays a
man who looks like Robert Montgomery, the film's star.
The book is set in Santa Fe during that city's most colorful time, the annual Labor Day weekend fiesta. Hughes
captures the city and its mixture of three cultures: In-
dian, Spanish, and "Gringo." Though some of the attitudes in the book seem a bit dated, i.e., the post World
War II mixture of cynicism and idealism, here, too, is a

book which has stood the difficult test of time.

Many writers of espionage are content to rely on newspaper stories thinly disguised as fiction, with terrorism and hijacking their stock in trade. Though Julian Symons' *The Broken Penny* (1953), reprinted by Carroll and Graf, $3.95, is flawed, it remains a much more imaginative cold-war thriller. Telling of the attempt to oust the communist government of a country never named, but apparently based on Poland, Symons provides a devastating picture of people under the totalitarian yoke, but he saves some room to show Britain and the British army in what is not their finest hour. There is suspense, but mostly *The Broken Penny* is about the attempt of its protagonist to maintain his idealism in a world that had gone mad in the early 1950s—and isn't much saner as I write these words.

If you somehow missed Ross Macdonald's *The Zebra-Striped Hearse* (1962) in its hardcover edition or in one of the previous twelve (!) Bantam printings, you get another chance, for that publisher has reprinted it again, after a four-year hiatus, at $3.95. Because this is one of the best in an outstanding series of private-eye novels, it is a book you shouldn't miss. You'll find many elements taken from the author's own life and placed into the investigation of his detective, Lew Archer, including the runaway father, the canyon forest fire, and California's unique culture, accurately presented in a book that ranges the state from Los Angeles to San Francisco. We see the compassion for which Archer is justifiably known, but there is also ample evidence of his intelligence as his creator has him quote Dante in a conversation so well written that it fits in seamlessly.

Holt, Rinehart, and Winston has reprinted most of the mysteries of Patricia Moyes in its Owl series, but I have not seen *Falling Star* yet. While it is not one of her stronger books, most other authors would be glad to claim it. Moyes had once been secretary to Peter Ustinov and had worked with him on the screenplay for *School for Scandal*. She knows movies, and that shows in every page of *Falling Star*. The motive and murder methods are not convincing, and the number of suspects too limited for a really strong puzzle. However, the author's experiment of eschewing third-person narration in favor of a story teller who is a movie executive and also a bit of a prig (and not too bright) works well. Also, Moyes's series detective, Henry Tibbett, continues to be likeable and efficient, if somewhat bland.

I suspect that detectives like Tibbett were a reaction to the eccentric sleuths of an earlier era, e.g., Holmes, Wolfe, and Poirot. John Creasey fathered a small army of detectives, all of whom had "smarts" and physical prowess, though none were especially colorful. Understandably, but perhaps unfairly, Creasey's name has often made mystery readers smile. The most prolific mystery writer, he started by writing some dreadful books in his early days. Not all were mysteries since he wrote in all genres. (One of his early "Tex Reilly" westerns is reputed to contain the deathless line about coyotes flying in the sky.) Creasey was best known for his George Gideon books, written under the J.J. Marric pseudonym, but G.G.'s roots were clearly in his older literary brother, Inspector Roger "Handsome" West, who appeared in forty-three novels and at least one short story. West started off rather inconspicuously in 1942, depending on a socialite friend for much of his detection and legwork. However, as the series progressed, Creasey's writing and West, as a hero, improved. Happily, Harper's Perennial Library has reprinted eight of the Roger West series, most at $3.95, and their selection is excellent, as witnessed by the following examples.

Serial killers are everywhere today. (I'm sure I pass them on the streets as I walk from the train to work.) *The Beauty Queen Killer* (1954) is a good early example, with some exciting scenes, marred only by difficult to accept motivation. *The Gelignite Gang* (1955) dates from the same year as the first Marric novel, and it also gives a good picture of London from a policeman's viewpoint. Here, the police are faced with a series of jewelry robberies, with the titular form of dynamite the common factor. When murder occurs during robbery in the city's largest department store, West is called in to solve a mystery that has more surprises than most. In *Death of a Postman* (1956) Creasey accomplishes what relatively few mystery writers do: he makes us *care* about the victim. A postal worker, who leaves behind a wife and five children, has been murdered during the Christmas rush. As we rapidly turn the pages of one of Creasey's best narratives, we become involved and want West to track down a particularly heinous killer.

THE BEST SHORT STORIES OF 1987

I read more than 300 mystery short stories published during the year, and, despite a few low points, I found variety and surprisingly high quality. Here are my annual choices, in order of preference:

1. **Robert Barnard**--"The Woman in the Wardrobe" (EQMM 12/87). A poignant tale in which there is an excellent reason for a man to turn amateur detective. Barnard gives a fine sense of Great Britain and a perfect ending to make this one of the best stories of recent years. The readers of EQMM also selected it as their favorite of the year, the first time my selection agreed with theirs.

2. **James Powell**--"Wingtips" (EQMM 6/87). An imaginative fairy tale of crime with the best puns, "those glorious flowers on the lawn of thought," since the heyday of Robert L. Fish.

3. **Joe Gores**--"Smart Guys Don't Snore" (*It's a Matter of Crime* #2). A fine first-person narrator plus genuine clues turn this into an outstanding blend of tough private eye and fair-play detection.

4. **Josh Pachter**--"Eighty Million Noses" (*Hardboiled* #7, Spring 1987). An hilarious parody of Ed McBain's 87th Precinct stories, one which captures their essence as no one (except McBain) has since Breen and Goulart did twenty years ago. A story which made me laugh out loud.

5. **Edward D. Hoch**--"Leopold and the Broken Bride" (EQMM 7/87). One of Hoch's best impossible crimes, as Captain Jules Leopold solves the case of a bride who disappears just as she is ready to march down the aisle.

6. **Jeffry Scott**--"The Best Kind of Lie" (*Prime Crimes* #5). A body buried for over forty years has been discovered, and a police inspector asks an old man to recall the days of "the Blitz." Good for its mood, good as history, and, most important, exceptionally good as mystery fiction.

7. **James Powell**--"The Tulip Juggernaut" (EQMM 9/87). Sgt. Maynard Bullock, RCMP, involved in preventing a wild plot to assassinate the Prime Minister of Canada and the President of the U.S. Besides good puns, here is a fine take-off of two unlikely bedfellows: operettas and terrorism.

8. **Robert Barnard**--"The Oxford Way of Death" (EQMM

4/87). Barnard in a much lighter vein than in his first-place story as he gives us a delightfully dry satire of British academia being dragged kicking and screaming into the twentieth century. After a murder, one elderly professor advises against ringing the police, saying, "if we can't settle a little matter like this without calling in outside authorities, what has become of academic freedom?"

9. **Stephen Wasylyk**--"The Search for Olga Bateau" (AHMM 11/87). Only a somewhat disappointing ending prevented this especially well-written story from being ranked even higher. At a time when so much fiction is predictable, it returns the *mystery* to the mystery.

10. **Edward D. Hoch**--"The Spy and the Short-Order Cipher" (EQMM 6/87). Because Rand's former boss keeps asking him favors, the reader gets one of the best code stories in years and another good example of fair-play detection within the limited space available in the short story.

11. **William F. Smith**--"An Almost Perfect Crime" (AHMM 4/87). An impossible-crime story of murder in a locked telephone booth, and a very good one indeed. The situation may be somewhat artificial, but the resolution is logical and fair, almost worthy of Hoch himself.

12. **James Powell**--"The Brim Whistle" (EQMM 2/87) Bullock again, and Powell turns the subject of Mounties' famous hats into comic crime.

13. **Josh Pachter**--"Chain Reaction" (*Espionage* 5/87). It was a good year for Pachter, who also edited *The Short Sheet* during 1987. Though its execution did not live up to the cleverness of its plot idea, this may have been the most original story of the year.

14. **Lawrence Doorley**--"Off and Running, Or, Bob Swillet's Luck (Bad)" (AHMM Mid-Dec 1987). Not truly a crime story, except in the broadest sense, but an extremely funny Horatio Alger parody.

Death of a Mystery Writer

Christiana Brand on March 11, 1988, in London at age 80. Known for both short stories (two of which won MWA Edgar nominations) and novels, she gained her greatest fame with her third mystery, *Green for Danger* (1944), a

superb detective story set in wartime Britain. The movie
version has been called one of the three best detective
films ever.   American mystery fans who attended
Bouchercon in 1976 and 1977 will also recall Mrs. Brand
as a delightful raconteur, in the school of such British
comediennes as Margaret Rutherford and Hermione
Gingold.

   I.A.L. Diamond on April 21, 1988, in Beverly Hills,
Calif., at age 67.   Though best known for such
screenplays as the Oscar-winning *The Apartment* and
Some Like It Hot, on which he collaborated with Billy
Wilder, Diamond occasionally wrote film scripts with a
mystery background. These included *The Private Life of
Sherlock Holmes* (with Wilder) and *Murder in the Blue
Room.*

   Randall Garrett on Dec. 31, 1987, in Texas at age 60.
He successfully combined mystery and science fiction in
the two books he wrote, in collaboration with Larry M.
Marks, about Lord Darcy: *Too Many Magicians* (1967) and
Murder and Magic (1979), a short-story collection.

   Veronica Parker Johns on April 14, 1988, in New York
City at age 81.   She was the author of five mystery
novels, the most famous of which were her last two,
Murder by the Day (1953) and *Servant's Problem* (1958),
both of which featured Webster Flagg, perhaps the first
serious black series detective.   Three times she won
second prizes in the annual short-story contests of
EQMM, with "The Homecoming" in the June 1952 issue an
especially memorable work.   Though she remained a
member of MWA, Johns' predominant interest during the
last quarter century of her life was sea shells. She was
president of the New York Shell Club and owned a store,
on Manhattan's East Side, in which she sold shells. Her
last book was the nonfictional *She Sells Sea Shells* (1968).

   Elizabeth Linington on April 5, 1988, in Los Angeles at
age 67.   She did not publish her first mystery until she
was 39, having first written five historical novels.   She
claimed she turned to the mystery, which she considered
a "modern morality play," when liberal editors insisted on
censoring her historical fiction.   Except for a suspense
novel written as Anne Blaisdell, Linington was best
known for more than seventy police-procedural mysteries
set in the Los Angeles area. (As Lesley Egan she created
attorney Jesse Falkenstein, but he frequently helps his
policeman friend, Sgt. Andy Clock.   Another Egan
character was Detective Vic Varallo of the Pasadena

police.)

Linington's first, and most famous, detective was Lt.
Luis Mendoza, a wealthy Los Angeles detective whose love
of solving mysteries and righting wrongs, rather than
money, kept him on the police force. She wrote about
him under the Dell Shannon pseudonym, beginning with
Case Pending (1960), probably the best book in a long
series. Under her own name she created a series involving Sgt. Ivor Maddox and policewoman Sue Carstairs of
Hollywood. Again, the early books in this series were
best, especially *Greenmask* (1964) with its use of the
mysteries of the golden age to help Maddox identify a
contemporary serial killer.

Extraordinarily prolific, Linington once claimed to
spend no more than few weeks on each of her books. (At
one time she was very active in the John Birch Society.)
Some critics found her procedurals lacked authenticity,
and, indeed, she admitted to not having visited any police stations. However, like her fellow procedural writer,
Creasey, she could create much sympathy for crime vic-
tims, and she was extremely popular and even one of the
few writers to have her own fan club.

Edward Mathis in Jan. 1988 in Euless, Texas. Though
he did not publish his first mystery until 1985, when he
was of advanced years and failing health, Mathis quickly
became very popular through his depiction of the Texas
scene and his series private eye, Dan Roman. MWA has
reported that he left behind 18 manuscripts, so it is
likely that his protagonist will outlive him for many years
to come.

George Sklar on May 15, 1988, in Los Angeles at age
79. He collaborated with Vera Caspary on *Laura,* the 1945
play based on her best-selling mystery. Blacklisted from
stage and screen writing because of his political views,
he became a novelist, writing a best-seller, *The Two
Worlds of Johnny Truro.*

Charles Willeford on March 27, 1988, in South Miami,
Florida, at age 69. Though he had written 13 prior
novels, Willeford established his reputation in the
mystery field only recently with his series about Hoke
Moseley of the Miami P.D., beginning with *Miami Blues*
(1984). *New Hope for the Dead* (1985), which nicely mixed
Moseley's personal problems with a crime story, is
considered by many to be the best of Willeford's mysteries.

Reel Murders: Cinevent 20
Walter Albert

The first person I ran into at the Columbus (Ohio) annual Memorial Day weekend film festival was Dan Stumpf--the best writer on American *film noir* whose work I am familiar with--who was smiling contentedly in the way we confirmed film junkies do after a particularly happy film experience. "You're going to like 'Super Sleuth,'" he whispered to me. (Film junkies never talk during film showings and, when they recommend a film, talk in a low voice so that the privileged information does not reach unfriendly ears.) "I hope so," I muttered distractedly, giving the appearance of receiving the tip without attaching undue importance to it since a film junkie would never want to appear to accept a recommendation for a film he might discover he loathes. Film junkies are generally skeptical before the fact and reticent after it. After all, we spent much of our formative movie years in a monogamous relationship with the silver screen and to admit a third participant to our rites has something of the adulterous about it.

But the film junkie is, at heart, an honest sort and I want to acknowledge publicly that Dan was right about "Super Sleuth." I did like it and this 1937 RKO release--which I finally saw at the end of the convention on Monday morning (the Monday morning films at the end of the convention are previewed on Friday afternoon for early arrivals and early departures)--was one of the high points of a convention I have been attending since 1980. The fact that this modest feature was a high point probably says something about the quality of the screenings I attended. There was, perhaps, nothing as abysmal as the "Gracie Allen Murder Case" I fled a few years ago, but there was nothing as riveting for me as the Lon Chaney features I look forward to and, in fact, there was no Lon Chaney film at all this year.

There was, however, an unusually high concentration of films featuring murder and crime. The film many of us were most eagerly anticipating was "The Bat Whispers" (United Artists, 1930; directed by Roland West), based on the Mary Roberts Rinehart-Avery Hopwood stage melodrama "The Bat." The film had been scheduled for 1987 but had failed to arrive. It was scheduled for a showing on Saturday at 10 p.m.—about half-way through the convention—and in the twenty-four hours leading up to it I had warmed the bench during eight films, for a total of 10 hours and fifty minutes, not counting the several animated short subjects that preceded several of the showings. Four of these were crime films of one sort or another, ranging from a modestly entertaining mix of college musical and murder ("College Scandal," 1935), efficiently directed by Elliot Nugent, to the uneven but interesting "Among the Living" (Paramount, 1941), directed by Stuart Heisler, director of "The Monster and the Girl" (Paramount, 1941). The film begins with a marvelous tracking shot, travelling from a gloomy mansion to a graveside burial service. There are at least two other scenes in the film that are also visually exciting. In the more memorable, Albert Dekker, playing the psychotic twin of a good/bad pairing, is tracked by an overhead camera shooting at an angle as he pursues an increasingly frightened woman along dark, deserted, rain-glistening back streets. The camera-work is intermittently superb; the back-lot theatrics of this Southern Gothic thriller are something else again in spite of an interesting cast, with Dekker flanked by three attractive actresses, Susan Hayward, Jean Phillips and Frances Farmer, with Phillips particularly effective as the girl pursued by Dekker. The program notes, written by William Everson, characterize this appropriately as a "blend of *film noir* and horror," but it's the *film noir* elements that are the more arresting.

Bessie Love is charming in the silent melodrama "Going Crooked," but conventioneers expecting the pre-code "Night Nurse" (Warner Bros., 1931), directed by William Wellman and starring Barbara Stanwyck, to be a sleazy delight in the manner of last year's "Baby Face" (1933), were probably disappointed to find Stanwyck upholding the moral standards of the nursing profession. Clark

Gable is effective as the vicious mastermind of a shady operation that brings out the virtuous best in nurse Stanwyck.

By the time the credits for "The Bat Whispers" flashed on the screen, I was ready for a transcendent experience but I found myself hard-put to stay awake through the plot detours of this moody but predictable "old house" mystery. Some of the camera work showing the Bat at work was deft but, if they recall the visuals of Fritz Lang, as the program notes claim, they recall them only intermittently and this film, like so much of the schedule for Cinevent 20, seemed either to be the harbinger of something better to come (as in "Among the Living") or a reminder of an already achieved success that was only imperfectly reflected in the later film.

It was with these moody, disillusioned thoughts that I slunk out of the screening room on Saturday, but two much happier later experiences restored some of my confidence in the popular films of the 1930s. The first screening on Sunday morning (at 9 a. m.) was the de-lightful "Murder on the Blackboard," the second of the Edna Mae Oliver/James Gleason Hildegarde Withers/In-spector Piper collaborations (1934, directed by George Archainbaud). "The Penguin Pool Murder" (1932) had been one of the pleasures of an earlier Cinevent and this sequel was even better, in large part because of a better script, less dependent on a clever but somewhat cute opening gambit. Edgar Kennedy was good as Gleason's flat-footed assistant, but he was even better in "Super Sleuth," the Paramount film recommended to me three days earlier by fellow film junkie Dan Stumpf.

Jack Oakie plays a popular film sleuth who tries to repeat his success on screen in an off-screen mystery, abetted by studio publicist Ann Sothern (trying to cover up his almost constant mishandling of his amateur sleuthing). For once, Kennedy comes off as a sympathe-tic, even competent professional undone by an in-competent amateur, even though the bumbling "Edgar" character lurks somewhere not too far from the surface. The heavy is Eduardo Cianelli, the unforgettable "assas-sin" of "Gunga Din," and the comic/suspenseful climax has a wax museum as the perfect setting for the conclusion of a film about on- and off-screen detecting.

"Super Sleuth" could also have been the perfect conclusion for Cinevent 80, the triumph of superb professionalism in elevating fluff with finesse to finely-

tuned fun, but I must also add that three films of un-
common distinction afforded me the most consistent
pleasure at the convention. William Powell, in "Love
Crazy" (MGM, 1941), took comic chances that I never saw
him take in any other film and brought them off trium-
phantly. Frank Capra was the masterful director of a
silent comedy/drama, "Submarine" (Columbia, 1928), and
Walter Huston was a memorable lawman in "Law and
Order" (Universal, 1932). This disguised version of the
Wyatt Earp/Clanton Bros. shootout was based on a novel
by William R. Burnett, with screen-writing credit given to
John Huston. Grim, uncompromising, without a wasted
frame. The casting (Harry Carey, Raymond Hatton,
Russell Simpson and, in small parts, Andy Devine and
Walter Brennan) was inspired. It was directed by Edward
L. Cahn and I must note that I was astonished by the
encounter at this convention with directors of whose
credits I was largely ignorant. But the work of directors
like Stuart Heisler, George Archainbaud, and Ben Stoloff
("Super Sleuth") reminded me that a reputation is not
always a demonstration of consistent achievement. And
that may be the most important element in the film
education that the usually interesting and sometimes
inspired programming of the Columbus Cinevents continues to be for me.

Short Takes: "The Secret Six" (MGM, 1931; dir. George
Hill). I stumbled onto the last half of this crime film in
Paris, while I was checking channels to find something
other than the French-dubbed American TV series that
seem to dominate French television. The film was shown
in the original English-language version and featured an
impressive cast: Wallace Beery, Clark Gable, Lewis Stone,
Jean Harlow, Ralph Bellamy, Marjorie Rambeau, and
Johnny Mack Brown in a non-Western role. Beery and
Stone form an unlikely pair as a crime Syndicate ganglord
and a crooked lawyer opposed by a masked group of
concerned citizens. Harlow is the good/bad girl and
Gable, the undercover agent working to dethrone Beery
and expose Stone. The pre-classic-period MGM films don't
turn up on American TV these days (another legacy of the
Turner buy-out of the MGM film library), and it was a
pleasure to see even part of this skilful thriller by
another director previously unknown to me. "Mickey's
Magical World" (Walt Disney Home Video, 1988). I am
ready to lead a boycott of Disney video products. I

bought this tape with the expectation of seeing the complete "Sorcerer's Apprentice" from "Fantasia" and, perhaps, some other classic Disney shorts featuring Mickey as a magician. I was appalled to be confronted with a series of hacked-up versions of some of Disney's finest shorts ("Magician Mickey," the astonishing—when it is presented in a complete version—"Thru the Mirror," "Lonesome Ghosts," and "The Band Concert") and an abbreviated "Sorcerer's Apprentice."   A showcase of animation excerpts but no substitute for the real thing. And the final indignity was a colorized, potted version of "Gulliver Mickey." A distressing note on which to end this column and, to counteract some of my indignation, I add the promise—or it is a threat?—to report in the next "Reel Murders" on recent reissues by MGM/UA of three films you probably won't find in your corner video store: "Doctor X" (Curtiz, 1932), in the rare two-strip color version; "Mark of the Vampire" (Browning, 1935); and (if I can find a replacement for the British 1964 "Devil Doll" I was inadvertently sent) "The Devil-Doll" (Browning, 1936).   And some further comments on "old house" mysteries.

MYSTERY MOSTS: REPETITIOUS TITLES

Repetition, as we all know, is as much the soul of fair·play Mystery as of advertising. In its latter role it is important to Mystery in attracting readers (beginning with the editors, who decide whether books are to be published), and some Mystery writers have used it to advantage in their titles. Lawrence Vail and Julian Symons hit upon possibly the best repetition, with their evocatively titled books, both *Murder! Murder!*

Other writers who doubled up on the use of Poe's key word include Alan MacKinnon, *Murder, Repeat Murder;* Neill Graham, *Murder, Double Murder;* Michael Halliday (and earlier H. Ashbrook), *Murder Makes Murder;* and M.G. Hugi, *Murder Begets Murder.* The allied word "kill" also found multiple double users, including: *Kill One, Kill Two* by W.W. Anderson; *Kill Once, Kill Twice* by Kyle Hunt, and *Kill, Sweet Charity, Kill* by J.J. Potter.

Predictably, most writer who used this technique did so only once, but there were more who did it twice than I expected, and even "triple doublers" such as Ellery Queen (*Double, Double; Blow Hot, Blow Cold* and *Who Spies, Who Kills*) and the Lockridges (*Catch As Catch Can,* a title also used by Charlotte Armstrong on an Ace Double, *First Come, First Kill* and *Foggy, Foggy Death*) are fairly common.

Frank Gruber (you can look 'em up) did it four times, as did the already mentioned Halliday. Halliday and Hunt (see above) were both Creasey pen names, and Creasey also did a pair with double titles under his own name (*So Young, So Cold, So Fair,* which is most unusual as a triple repetition) and another pen name, Jeremy York (*To Kill or To Die*), for a leading total of at least seven usages of double titles. (Jeff Banks)

The Backward Reviewer
William F. Deeck

Frank Kane. *Esprit de Corpse*. Dell, 1965, 157 pages.

Yes, there's nothing new in one individual taking on the crooks and corrupt officials in a city. And it's been done better and in greater depth--*The Fools in Town Are on Our Side* and *Red Harvest* come immediately to mind. Nonetheless, this thriller is quite satisfactory for the second rank.

When a private eye, out of his depth, gets framed for murder in the sleazy Barbary Coast of Carsonette City in Southern California and is, with the eager assistance of his estranged wife, doomed to spend his life in the loony bin, he asks his partner to call in another private eye, Johnny Liddell. His partner--a she, although by no means another V.I. Warshawski--flies to New York to enlist Liddell's help. Apparently she goes in person since her argument isn't a strong one and she must compensate by "the hemispherical roundness of her full breasts." Upon viewing them, even clothed, Liddell's jaw drops and his good judgment vanishes. She knows her man.

(Has there ever been a female client in private-detective literature who had "empty" breasts? Have no tough PI's been weaned?)

Though threatened and attacked by the crooks and threatened and arrested by the corrupt police, Liddell emerges triumphant. He understands, and I'm taking his word for it, why the frame took place and how the bookies and the Mafia were being taken by other crooks.

As an added attraction, one of the villains ostensibly is a closet Edgar Wallace reader. When Liddell catches this desperado in a felonious act, the man says: "Okay, Mac. It's a fair cop."

Thomas Brace Haughey. *The Case of the Invisible Thief.* Bethany Fellowship, 1978, 159 pages.

The intelligence behind Sleuths, Ltd., a consulting detective firm at No. 31 Baker Street, London, is Geoffrey Weston, grandson of Mycroft Holmes. He and his colleague, John Taylor, Esq., are asked to investigate a theft at the Pinehurst Laboratory. In a building under constant surveillance by guards, infrared detectors, and closed-circuit television, a thief has managed to remove top-secret papers from a safe, the combination of which is known to only one person. A videotape from the closed-circuit TV focused on the safe shows that no one had opened it.

Like his great-uncle, Weston is a crackerjack scientist. He is also a born-again Christian. Both of these attributes play a role in his solving the case.

As a scientific illiterate, I got lost in the explanation of how the thief became invisible, although I suspect Weston's solution is science fictional rather than science. The villain is even more unlikely—some would say frankly impossible—under the tenets of many current theologies.

Not a badly written novel, but it probably should be read only by those who will read anything tangentially Holmesian and by those interested in religion in the mystery who are willing to accept the author's ground rules.

Clifford Knight. *The Affair of the Fainting Butler.* Dodd, Mead, 1943; Detective Book Club, 1943, 212 pages.

There are those, and I am among them, who read mysteries primarily to find out if the butler did indeed do it. Unfortunately, these days there are few novels in which you can suspect the butler, a breed that has been an endangered and even vanishing species for years. This is one of the old-fashioned novels that still affords us that pleasure. And, yes, the butler does faint. In fact, he faints three times. Did he do it? That would be telling.

Larry Weeks, agent—or flesh peddler, if you prefer—for Jenifer Janeway, who wrote magazine serials "that

made worrying wives, whose husbands had young sophis-
ticated secretaries, think of Reno," goes to Janeway's
home to try to keep her from carrying out her threat to
commit suicide. She is about to start writing screenplays,
and she is his meal ticket.

While Janeway and Weeks are in her garden, Sloan
Hinckley, Shakespearean actor and Weeks's other but
lesser client, appears on the wall. He is Janeway's
neighbor--ah, coincidence, where would mystery writers
be without you?--and has come to report that he has
discovered a corpse on her grounds. No corpse, however,
is to be found. When Janeway is visited shortly there-
after by an old friend, Hinckley claims that the old friend
was the corpse.

There are several murders of varying unlikelihood for
equally unlikely reasons. The amateur detective, Prof.
Huntoon Rogers, is a veritable nonentity. Though he is
present throughout the novel and solves the crimes, if
his name isn't before you at all times, you tend to forget
his existence.

Constance and Gwenyth Little. *The Black Shrouds.*
Doubleday, 1941; Collins, 1941; Popular Library No. 112,
no date, 190 pages.

To find fame--her father already has a fortune--on
the stage, Diana Prescott has come to New York City.
What she discovers, however, is horror at Mrs. Markham's
boarding house, which is occupied by the usual oddities
one finds at fictional boarding houses and maybe even at
the real ones. Two elderly and old-maid sisters, an
absolutely harmless pair, are found murdered--blud-
geoned and then gassed.

It's obvious it's an inside job, but the police, in more
ways than one, haven't a clue. Even when another
resident disappears and items appear and disappear and
books and other objects are burnt in the furnace, the
officials are at a loss. Though frightened a fair part of
the time, Prescott does her own investigating, primarily
to avoid playing bridge with her father.

For reasons unknown, but perhaps because the
inhabitants are generally eccentrics, I enjoy mysteries
with boarding-house settings. I'd have enjoyed this one
anyhow because the Littles are quite amusing writers and
their Miss Giddens is a delightfully nutty character. And

if my recommendation isn't enough, I refer you to *Something Wicked,* by Carolyn G. Hart, in which her wonderful bookstore, Death on Demand (Annie Laurence, prop.), put *The Black Shrouds* in its window with several other books to illustrate humor in the mystery.

Ellery Queen.   *The Scarlet Letters.*   Little, Brown, 1953; Gollancz, 1953; in *The New York Murders,* Little, Brown, no date, 126 pages.

Dirk Lawrence, not too successful mystery writer and even less successful "serious" writer, and his rich wife, Martha, have a perfect marriage. Perfect, that is, until Dirk begins to suspect that his wife is cuckolding him and becomes drunken and violent. Nikki Porter, Ellery Queen's secretary, is a friend of Martha's. Despite his quite correct protests that he is no good at such things, she gets Queen involved in the domestic discord.

Queen does a lot of running around and very little deducing. As a private-eye type, he's futile, and he admits it. Private eyes "tail" people; Queen "trails" them.

It is evident to anyone with the meanest intelligence—which this reader possesses on a good day—what the outcome of this case will be. So with vast anticipation the reader waits for Ellery Queen the author's twist, the final surprise, the revelation that nothing is what it seems. Most surprisingly, the shock is that everything is indeed exactly what it seems.

Those who have knowledge of the Queen saga may recall an earlier novel in which Biff Barnes or Barnes Biff or Beau Rummell or someone with a name like that, a partner with Queen in an investigative agency, pretended he was Ellery Queen. That, I believe, is what happened here, without Ellery Queen the author bothering to reveal it. Good lord, even Sergeant Velie could have figured out the dying message the moment it was written, yet this Ellery Queen dithers about it for days.

Nonetheless, despite the obviousness of the plot and Queen the detective's dimwittedness, there's an engrossing novel here.

Jack S. Scott. *The Poor Old Lady's Dead.* Harper & Row, 1976, 151 pages; Hale, 1976, as *Dead Poor Old Lady.*

The Chief Inspector had come down with a bug and the Superintendent was not aware of it until Detective Inspector Rosher had taken over the investigation. So the tumble down the stairs by a little old lady at the Haven, an old folks' home, remains in the ham-fisted hands of Old Blubbergut, as he is unaffectionately known to his colleagues and his underlings.

Rosher has to deal with an alderman who is the dead lady's nephew and quite influential in the town, and finesse and subtlety are not Rosher's strong points, if they are points of his at all. A subplot involves Rosher's unhappy and hapless assistant, who has to suffer not only from his superior's taunts but from the demands of a pregnant mistress who, quite reasonably, wants him to leave his wife and marry her.

Rosher can be compared with Chief Inspector Wilfrid Dover in some ways, only Dover is a caricature, a grotesque, and funny. Rosher is unfunny and very close to real. He toadies to his superiors. As for his underlings, "Strangely, he was not unpopular with the rank and file, provided they were on a lowly rung and unlikely to rise far above it." Like Dover, he cadges meals and drinks from the unfortunate juniors who have to work with him. His personal habits aren't very pleasant, either.

As some other authors before him have discovered when they made their main character unpleasant, a continuing character must receive some empathy from the reader or be a burlesque like Dover. Otherwise, the normal reader will not buy further books in the series. Scott made Rosher more appealing and more human, though still not particularly pleasant, as the series advanced. Read this first recorded case of Rosher for a good investigation, some rather bitter humor, and to discover what he was like in the beginning. Then read the rest of Scott's novels featuring Rosher. They become even more enjoyable as Rosher mellows somewhat.

Milton K. Ozaki. *The Dummy Murder Case.* Graphic Books, 1951, 190 pages.

As part of Professor Caldwell's class in psychology, the Professor plans a visual demonstration to instruct on perceptual responses. Instead of the usual classroom show, a rather complex presentation is given to the class outdoors: Two friends of the Professor's assistant, Bendy, stage a mock murder, with a young lady being shot at the end of a pier and falling into the water. A mannequin has already been sunk at the spot. The police, with prior arrangement, are to come and drag for the body.

Instead of finding the mannequin, the draggers recover the body of a young woman with her throat slit. The police report to Caldwell that the woman had no visible means of support--and no visible person to support her--and has in her apartment a room equipped like the wrapping department of a store, with paper from several first-class establishments and totally empty boxes already wrapped. If there were no other reason for him to investigate, this puzzle would bring Caldwell into the case, despite the objections of Bendy, who knows he will have to do all the work while the Professor does the thinking.

There are enough coincidences in the novel to keep a reader muttering, "It's a small world" or maybe even "It's an infinitesimal world." Only an interest in the explanation for the wrapped empty boxes kept me reading to the end.

Robert Edmond Alter. *Carny Kill.* Fawcett Gold Medal, 1966, 160 pages; Black Lizard Books, 1986.

Let me state at the beginning that a novel of this type is not my customary reading of choice. Still, I was glad I read it. Alter has presented an absorbing setting and an engrossing albeit not wholly admirable main character.

Leslie M. Thaxton, who prefers to be called Thax, seeks employment at Neverland in Florida, a borrowing of the Disneyland idea. This was, of course, before the construction of Disney World. One of the attractions is an old-fashioned carnival, and Thaxton, who has been a barker and prestidigitator, fits right in at the shell-game stand.

Unfortunately, the owner of Neverland has married Thaxton's former wife, a beautiful but unpleasant woman with a "cold, sensual, calculating look" who is a former knife thrower and has used Thax as an unwitting target. Even more unfortunately, the morning after Thaxton's arrival his new boss is found among the alligators where the Swamp Ride is located, with one of his wife's knives in his back.

Thaxton is a suspect, along with his former wife. The evidence that she did it is so overwhelming that it is obvious that she didn't do it. Luckily for her, a policeman with imagination is in charge and recognizes a frame-up.

As pointed out previously, Thaxton is a most interesting character, with both depths and shallows. Well read in the earlier adventure-type literature—particularly Robert Louis Stevenson—and intelligent, he also has a considerable chip on his shoulder and, whether the author intended it or not, is obviously a loser. He's something of a philosopher, too, yet cannot see the parallel between his observations, "She smiled at both of us—a real earthy we-know-what-god-put-it-there-for-don't-we-boys smile. She was about as tarty as they come," and "I like bed. I like the female form. I damn well like the lust of female flesh—in bed, out of bed, anywhere."

Fawcett published this novel in those more innocent days when the "f" word was still being blanked out—presumably Black Lizard restores the missing letters—and the sex is suggested rather than explicit. (I will spare you my lecture as to how a useful word like "f———ing" has been so abused both orally and in print that it has become merely a weak and undefinable intensifier like "very.")

If you can accept Thaxton's double standard, and even if you can't, you should find this gripping reading.

Milton Propper. *The Great Insurance Murders*. Harper, 1937; Harrap, 1938; Prize Mystery Novels No. 7, 1943, 128 pages.

While seated on a horse during a polo game, Bruce Clinton is shot in the head by a gunman using a .38 automatic with silencer from "less than 200 feet." "A neat shot, but not too skillful, after all," Tommy Rankin, Homicide Squad detective, opines. Hard man to impress, I'd opine.

"By a system of trial and error, he [Rankin] ultimately cleared up his problems, sometimes even blundering into the answer." In this novel he is convinced at various times that three separate people were the murderer. Luckily, he does blunder into the answer, leaving profuse loose ends.

Should anyone have an urge to read a Milton Propper mystery, this is probably not the one to choose.

Parenthetically, certain low-level detectives and obvious crooks say "yu," sometimes, in place of "you." Could a kindly Philadelphian, since that city is where this novel takes place, explain the difference in pronunciation?

Whitman Chambers. *Dead Men Leave No Fingerprints.* Doubleday, 1935; Cassell, 1935; Caxton House, 1939, 298 pages.

Danish film star and sexpot Hilda Haan hires private detective Stanton Lake to get her out of the clutches of a man who threatens to tell her studio about her "moral turpitude" unless she marries him. Lake says he'll get her out of the mess if he has to kill the man to do it.

That turns out to be unnecessary. Someone else does the job for him while preparations are being made for a séance at the residence of Rufus Raybourne, a real-estate magnate now suffering hard times. The victim is killed with a poker that has on it the fingerprints of an enemy of Raybourne's. Yet this enemy died more than a year earlier in prison. Or did he? Lake plays ghoul and finds an empty grave.

Two more murders take place. After each one, the same fingerprints are found.

An unusual motive, a cunning--well, he or she would have been if the killings hadn't continued once Lake's identity was revealed--murderer, and an interesting character in Lake. The writing level is the '30s standard: Passable.

Will Creed. *Death Comes Grinning.* Five Star Mystery, 1946, 125 pages; Edwards, 1947.

> Oh, Pittsburgh's the home of the steel mill,
> The home of the rail and the rod;
> Where the Cooks speak only to Bodemans
> And the Bodemans speak only to God.

Yes, I know you've heard it with different names, but never mind. Sally Brown, recently graduated nurse, is hired to care for the relict of Cyrus Bodeman, who spoke, it would seem, more with Satan than God. Brown is chosen because of her name, which implies to some person or persons unnamed, for reason or reasons unspecified, and in this case downright erroneously, plainness in appearance. Why this is important the author sayeth not.

Bodeman's widow is no prize, either, nor are her three sons. An unpleasant family, an unpleasant house, and Mrs. Bodeman has $100,000 in cash hidden away. She knows someone is trying to kill her for the money and the inheritance, so she gives Brown the key to the money box and names her in her will to get whatever else there is except the house. Mrs. Bodeman likes Brown. It's a good thing she didn't hate her.

After the housekeeper dies suspiciously, Brown investigates. This requires her tasting a substance that could be strychnine and fortunately isn't. She later, again voluntarily, drinks from a glass with a substance that could be strychnine and is. Two glasses of water drunk in quick succession, the popular and seemingly efficacious antidote to strychnine poisoning, save her for further folly.

This is primarily a suspense novel, as you will have noted, and not a very good one, as I will note for you. Nobody gets the house or the money; Brown gets and deserves one of the Bodeman boys.

Lyon Mearson. *Phantom Fingers*. Macaulay, 1927, third printing 1929, 256 pages; Hutchinson, 1929.

Damon Knight, I believe it was, once reviewed what he called an "idiot novel," wherein the hero was an idiot and the heroine was an idiot, but fortunately the villain was a superidiot. This novel qualifies for that description.

The Grand Theatre in New York City is about to put on a new play. The management and the two stars receive threatening letters—signed variously "Pro Bono Publico," "Constant Reader," and "A Well-Wisher," affording the only intentional humor in the novel. If the male lead attempts to make love to the female star on the stage, he is doomed, says the threatener.

The play takes place, and the male star does indeed die, being strangled and then having his neck broken by some invisible agency in full view of the audience and almost in full view of the detective in the case, Steve

Muirhead, who would have seen it from the beginning if he had been paying attention.

Muirhead is more alert on the second occasion when an understudy takes over the role and begins being choked on stage, again by an invisible hand. With a visible knife Muirhead stabs the invisible hand and saves the understudy's life. Does Muirhead remember his brave and intelligent—his only one—act? No. He puts the knife away somewhere safe and is thus at the mercy of the villain.

Murder and attempted murder, and Muirhead is the sole policeman involved in the investigation. The rest of the force is directing traffic, one gathers. "A fate worse than death" is mentioned often enough in regard to the heroine to make one suspect that the author was trying to titillate his readers since he couldn't entertain them.

The only mysteries worth thinking about here are how Muirhead's man Briggs becomes Muirhead's man Grigson a few pages later and how this wretched amalgamation of mystery and science fiction went into a third printing. How it got published originally I will let others ponder.

Stanley Casson. *Murder by Burial*. H. Hamilton, 1938; Harper, 1938; Penguin Books, Third Printing, 1946, 238 pages.

Col. Theodore Cackett, R.E., D.S.O., has formed in Kynchester the Roman Guard for the Regeneration of Britain and is now planning erect a monument to the memory of the Emperor Claudius in recognition of the civilizing influence that the Romans brought to the Isles. On the other hand, Canon Burbery knows that the early Britons were a great deal more civilized than commonly supposed. It is his plan to begin an archaeological dig to prove that Kynchester was the stronghold of King Cunobeline (or Cymbeline, as Shakespeare would have it). He hopes that the citizens of the city will take the claims in behalf of the Romans less seriously after they have been shown their heritage.

A rivalry of this sort is bound to create bad feelings. Add to it the Canon's blackballing of Cackett at the learned Augusteum Club and Cackett's becoming involved in a plot to arm the landowners of England to defend against a possible revolution, and anything can happen. In this case, a death occurs. Following a fortuitous investigation by a professional archaeologist, questions are raised whether the death was indeed "an act of God."

Well written, quite literate, amusing in parts, informative on both archaeology and numismatics. The dialogue sometimes seems more lecture than conversation, but the lectures are interesting and thus tolerable.

Fascinating also is Miss Boddick's expatiation on Holmes's view of the country as a scene of crime: "You Londoners will never realise the depths of depravity of the countryside.... Why, the English countryside is one congealed mass of intrigue and petty spite. That is why almost every murder story is placed in a country town or in some remote village, where all the natural passions have free play."

George Childerness. *Murder in False Face.* Phoenix Press, 1943; Hangman's House, no date, "condensed slightly," 120 pages.

Chet Phelps, assistant to Mr. Kent, first name undisclosed but publisher of twenty-odd newspapers, has some unusual duties. Preventing his boss from starving himself in the name of economy is foremost, but he also does some "stenography, reporting, killing of snakes (Denver), subornation of perjury (Milwaukee) and grave robbery in a southern city."

After an evening of gambling and drinking, Phelps wakes up the next morning in bed with a young lady whose father had sued Kent for libel. Worse, Phelps discovers that during the night, a total blank to him, he married the young lady, her father had been murdered, probably strangled but also shot twice and horribly mutilated, after which the murderer had painted a false face on what was left of the corpse's real face.

As usual, there are lots of suspects, all of whom seem to have been busy getting in each other's way at the scene of the crime. Phelps investigates, when he isn't busy getting sloshed. However, it is Kent, who has an odd fascination for waxing his nails, who discovers the murderer.

Nothing special here, though it has its amusing moments. Childerness wrote one more mystery, *Too Many Murderers* (1944); maybe he got better.

Rufus King. *Design in Evil.* Doubleday, 1942; Popular
Library, no date, 158 pages.

At the moment astrology is being ridiculed, deservedly
to be sure. Even when at astrology's beginning the
horoscopes were cast correctly, the success rate of the
predictions was no better than random chance. Yet many
who disdain astrology accept psychiatry, with an equally
dubious claim to scientific validity and a prediction rate
no better, and possibly worse, than astrology.
   Dr. Crowninshield, an authority in the psychiatric area
who has reached an age and a level of experience that
allows him to abandon doubt and uncertainty, has con-
cluded, after no examination whatsoever, that Miriam Lake
is really Jennifer Murcheson, wealthy and very peculiar
even when normal, who mysteriously left her ranch in
California and is now suffering from schizophrenia.
Crowninshield's assistant, Dr. Stone, is also convinced
that Lake is Murcheson, but he is certain she is faking
the alleged illness.
   By some dastardly plotting and a little arson, the
Murcheson family--uncle, aunt, and cousin--get Lake
aboard their yacht en route to the Caribbean. Ostensibly
the purpose is to effect a cure. Lake, however, begins to
realize that it is someone's design to murder her at sea
in order to gain the real Murcheson's fortune. With the
"scientists" aboard the vessel having their minds made
up, her claims and attempts at proof are ignored. Thus
her situation is both frustrating and perilous.
   The more I read of Rufus King's novels, the more I am
impressed by their general high level. His plotting is
usually first class, the atmosphere of menace is almost
always well done, his suspects are often few, something
appreciated by this feeble-minded reader, and the clues
are generally fair. While he has a weakness for polysyl-
lables, so do I. Characterization sometimes is a bit weak,
but King often makes up for it by his humor. In this
novel, Lake's amusing comments in the face of her
obvious danger keep the novel from becoming just
another damsel-in-distress type.

Verdicts
(Book Reviews)

Tony Hillerman. *A Thief of Time.* Harper & Row, 1988, 209 pp.

The world needs another review of Tony Hillerman's latest and greatest success like it needs another plug for Roger Rabbitt, but this Southwestophile feels compelled to add to the redundancy. This review, however, is totally personal and barely critical. To someone who loves that country and such of its legends and beauty as short visits have made possible, the professional critics' comments about the eery setting, the likable characters, and the satisfying twists in the plot seem as inadequate as the flowery descriptions in program notes that attempt to describe a symphony. Yes, yes, Hillerman is at his best here making both of his regular series police officers real, gutsy, and sympathetic; yes, the weaves a fine yarn; yes, his interlocking of native culture and Anglo intrusion works. But what is most effective is how the real places, customs, and events make verisimilitude an unnecessary word.

Among the truly real descriptions familiar to this reviewer are these that wring truth and joy from every page: magnificent Chaco Canyon where Fajada Butte and the pueblo ruins jar the visitor with the calling spirits of the Anasazi; Navajo hogans on the canyon floors where tamarisk branches sway in the wind; the clay roads that are impossibly rutted in the dry weather and dangerously slick in the rain; petroglyphs and petrographs scratched on or painted in the "desert varnish" on the canyon walls; the humorous but wily figure of Kokopelli, the hunchbacked flute player, present in most of the myster-

ious displays of that art on the walls; even the funda-
mentalist Christian tent-revival preacher shouting in
Navajo over a public-address system.   Surely, too,
Lieutenant Joe Leaphorn and Officer Jim Chee of the
Navajo Tribal Police are really there thanklessly fighting
crime and loneliness in humane ways.

As the prestigious critics point out, Hillerman uses the
setting to its best advantage. As the writers of Westerns
have found, too, the difficulties of quick and clear
communication make for more suspense. If only Jim Chee
had a phone in his trailer.... If only it were not so far
from Window Rock, Arizona, to Bluff, Utah.... Still, there
is much more to recommend *A Thief of Time* than the
technical expertise of the writer who values more his
praise from the Navajo Tribe than his Edgar from the
Mystery Writers of America. The last conversation of the
book is simple and should not be surprising; yet, it is
extraordinarily moving.   The plot, the characterization,
the setting are all intertwined in that final request. One
more touch that makes the book such a personal pleasure.
(Martha Alderson)

Tony Hillerman.   *The Dark Wind.*   Harper & Row, 1982;
     Avon, 1983.
Tony Hillerman. *Skinwalkers.* Harper & Row, 1986; Peren-
     nial, 1987.

Tony Hillerman is probably writing the best mysteries
in America today.   He has taken the deserts and
mountains of the Southwest as his territory, and the
Navajo Tribal policemen, Officer Jim Chee and Lt. Joe
Leaphorn, as his protagonists. He brings the beauties
and dangers of that land into our living-rooms, and the
Navajo heritage becomes more understandable as part of
the inclusive American culture.

The Navajo believe that persons need to be in
harmony, with themselves and the natural world. When
they are not, they may be sick or do strange things. A
traditional Navajo, feeling him-or-herself out of harmony,
will seek a "sing," a ceremonial done by a shaman, a
singer who knows the traditional chants and sand
paintings by heart. Jim Chee is learning to be a singer,
under the tuition of his maternal uncle. Chee has a
degree in anthropology and could work in the white
culture, but despite his love for white teacher Mary

Landon, he is bound by strong ties to the land between the Sacred Mountains and to Navajo ways.

As in any society, there are evil Navajos; they are witches, the skinwalkers. They can blow a little bead of bone into the person they want to harm, and that person will sicken and die. Chee and Leaphorn often must deal with people who believe in witchcraft and who act accordingly. Often they must take this into consideration in their investigations. In *The Dark Wind* a Navajo man is found dead near a Hopi ceremonial trail. The skin of his hands and feet had been stripped off, a mark of witchcraft. At about the same time a plane crashes in the desert, led by misplaced landing lights. Its cargo, probably cocaine, is missing. Chee was in the vicinity, investigating the vandalism of a windmill. These three apparently unrelated events are peculiarly linked. That linkage leads Chee into conflict with the U.S. Drug Enforcement Agency personnel. At the last it takes him to a secret Hopi ceremony where the kachinas walk, along with evil beings.

Skinwalkers confronts the belief in witchcraft directly. Joe Leaphorn is troubled by three murders in Navajo territory; though the FBI is theoretically in charge, he looks for connections. When Jim Chee's trailer is blasted by a shotgun, hitting the bunk he'd just left, coincidence seems too long an arm. For the first time, Chee and Leaphorn work together, not entirely comfortably and trustingly.

Their private anxieties enter into this book, making both rounded people with whom we can empathize. Mary Landon is off in Wisconsin at college, and she's not going to return for the break they'd planned to spend together. Their tie is thinning, and Chee is lonely. Leaphorn's beloved wife of many years, Emma, is showing all the signs of Alzheimer's Disease, and the pain of this at times almost overwhelms him.

Navajo justice is not always the same as white-man's justice. Navajo values are not the white-man's values. Hillerman, himself white, has so penetrated the native-American worldview that he can present it to us lovingly, as inevitably right for these people and that place. Paradoxically, Hillerman's books, which are taut and suspenseful, also enable us to feel the value of slowing down and paying full attention to our surroundings.

And, yes, Chee and Leaphorn find out who is killing people in a seemingly random way, and why. The real "witch" is uncovered without doing violence to Navajo values. (Maryell Cleary)

William X. Kienzle. *Deadline for a Critic.* Andrews, McMeII & Parker, 1987; Ballantine, 1988.

An aging gay music and theater critic, fired from his prestigious job on a New York City daily, becomes critic for a small Detroit paper. His poison-dipped typewriter keys and poisonous whisperings into influential ears have done irreparable damage to those he considers his foes. Now, diabetic and with AIDS, he is gorging himself with rich food and drink while once more writing vitriolic lines after a chamber-music concert. In the audience are others he has harmed; all have written him recently to tell him off. So, when his overtaxed heart gives out after he reads their letters, is it murder? Well, Detroit's finest and Father Koesler seem to think so. Koesler, as an old school friend of the deceased, celebrates the funeral Mass. While the Mass goes on, we readers are given a tour of the past through Koesler's mental flashbacks. We learn just how eminently murderable this man was. The biggest question throughout the book is not whodunit, but why didn't someone do it long ago? (Maryell Cleary)

Carolyn G. Hart. *Design for Murder.* Bantam, 1988.

Murder parties are all the rage. So the Chastain (SC) Historical Preservation Society is throwing one as part of its annual house-and-garden tour. Annie Laurence of the Death on Demand bookstore is tapped to organize and administer it, for a fee. Historic Chastain has a grand dame, Corinne Prichard Webster, who runs the Society, the town, and would like to run Annie as well. Before the first of the three Murder Nights is over, Corinne has taken a part in a real murder. Since Annie is the ideal candidate for first murderer, outsider that she is, she and fiancé Max Darling must collaborate to solve the crime. The task is not easy. Chastain is crowded with tourists, and Annie's customers are clamoring for their favorite authors' books; the show, of course, must also go on. With Corinne's family and presumed friends agonizing and accusing Annie, she must look for clues to the actual murder while keeping the fictional murder undercover.

The logistics of the Murder Nights seem impossible to this observer, in spite of maps to orient oneself by. Other than that, there's much to enjoy. The names of many mystery authors drop from Annie's lips just as they did in *Death on Demand*, the first book about this attractive amateur detective. This time there's a wedding in view at the end. (Maryell Cleary)

Joan Hess. *The Murder at the Murder at the Mimosa Inn.* St. Martin's Press, 1986; Ballantine, 1987.

Murder parties are all the rage. So Harmon Crundall, amateur actor and holder of the option on the Mimosa Inn, thinks it would be neat to have a Murder Weekend at the inn. Its struggling proprietors aren't so sure, but go along. Claire Malloy, bookstore owner and widowed mother of teen-aged Caron, goes along for the fun and challenge, hoping to win the champagne prize. The dramatic group has planned a murder, complete with cryptic clues. But the fun and games are interrupted by, you guessed it, a real murder. Lt. Peter Rosen, who is ardently pursuing Claire, is there in his professional as well as his personal capacity, competing with Claire both in the game and in solving the actual crime. Fourteen-year-old Caron is bored but willing to help—with a little bribery—on the word-puzzle clues. Confusion often reigns, as the roles are hard to disentangle from reality. A light and generally amusing read, with a sympathetic trio who seem likely to become series characters. (Maryell Cleary)

Peter Lovesey. *The False Inspector Dew.* Pantheon, 1982.

Abandoning Sgt. Cribb for the nonce, Lovesey brings us a non-series mystery in a light vein. The time is 1921; the scene a transatlantic liner; the problem, a woman overboard and drowned. The captain calls on Inspector Dew, traveling second class, to investigate. The only trouble is that the real Inspector Dew is home in England, retired, while someone else has taken his name for the voyage. The real Inspector Dew is renowned for catching Dr. Crippen and Ethel LeNeve in the well-known wife-murder of years before. The false Inspector Dew himself has murder on his mind. With a lively cast, a totally unexpected body, and both romance and money on the minds of quite a few of those on board, there's an exciting time to be had. Surprises abound. This is an offbeat delight for Lovesey admirers as well as for first-time readers of his work. (Maryell Cleary)

P.M. Carlson. *Murder Unrenovated.* (A Maggie Ryan Mystery—Maggie Ryan 1972.) Bantam, 1988.

Carlson has taken the unusual step of dating the books in this series, so one can readily see where each fits in; this also keeps one from confusing the copyright date with the time in which she has set her books. Since these are relatively recent times, this is helpful. Actor Nick O'Connor and statistician Maggie Ryan have appeared in three previous mysteries. The books have brought them from first meeting to the stage they're in in this book, married and pregnant. Now living in New York, they set out to find a city house they can renovate and live in, one they can afford. What they find is an old brownstone with great possibilities, but complete with dead body and extremely lively and recalcitrant tenant. Julia Northrup, the sixty-ish woman who refuses to vacate her basement apartment and tries to fend off potential buyers in creative ways, promptly takes over the book. She is widowed, unconventional, gutsy, and a joy. Her curiosity about the murdered young man whose body is found on the top floor makes her vulnerable. Her courage, her flair, her willingness to take risks endear her to readers. O'Connor and Ryan are their usual inquisitive, tenacious selves, but Northrup is the star. May we hear more about her as the O'Connor-Ryan saga goes on. (Maryell Cleary)

P.M. Carlson. *Audition for Murder.* Avon, 1985.

Read this one first if you can. In it Nick O'Connor has a wife, and her name is Lisette. They are the professional leads in a college production of Hamlet. Very quickly we learn that Lisette is depressed, drinking herself into a stupor, even suicidal; later on we find out why. Playing Ophelia is supposed to be therapeutic for her, but the mad scene is an unnerving challenge. And accidents keep happening, always to Lisette. Maggie

Ryan, one of the student actors, turns detective when the murder occurs. Cast and crew include some interesting characters; significant clues are seeded into the plot; the suspense is strong, especially if you haven't read others in this series. But if you have, read it anyway; it's a good story on its own and it gives background for the continuing characters. (Maryell Cleary)

Stephen Youngkin, James Bigwood, and Raymond Cabana, Jr. *The Films of Peter Lorre* Citadel, 1982.

In 1931 a young, unknown actor mesmerized movie audiences all over the world with his volatile performance as a child-murderer in the German classic thriller "M."

This was the beginning of Peter Lorre's knotty career on the silver screen. In spite of international fame and some unique contributions to the medium, he was never again able to attain the artistic heights of his initial effort.

The authors of *The Films of Peter Lorre* theorize that the actor's portrayal "signaled the arrival of a new type of killer, infinitely more horrifying in his ordinariness. It typecast him for life."

Not unlike Bela Lugosi and Boris Karloff, the kings of horror film, who yearned for a more meaningful acting career but were fated to be stamped as Dracula and the Frankenstein monster, respectively, Peter Lorre too is mostly remembered for his stints in various movies of stark menace. The authors of this in-depth investigation have spent eight years interviewing more than two hundred of the actor's relatives, friends and co-workers.

In a lengthy biographical introduction we learn that Lorre's birthplace foreshadowed his future image. The Carpathian mountains have given birth to the legends of vampires and werewolves.

Lorre's beginnings were far less phantasmic. His real name was Ladislav Lowenstein, and he was the grandson of a rabbi.

His father, a hard-working commercial manager, was displeased when the wayward son announced that he wanted to become an actor. Considered the black sheep of the family, Peter migrated to Vienna penniless and malnourished, sleeping on park benches.

Vienna then was the focal point of cultural activity. The enterprising young man managed to get a job as a claquer (applauder planted to assure a standing ovation), thus was admitted to theatres free.

Eventually he joined an improvisational theatre, in which he created his own stories and dialogue. He received no formal training, but for his acting technique he looked within, exploring and probing the human condition.

With the newly acquired stage name of Peter Lorre, the fledgling professional moved from one company to another, appearing in a series of children's productions and in touring groups.

After a while, he moved to Berlin, where he struck the fancy of Bertolt Brecht due to his offbeat, diminutive appearance, and began to make a name for himself in a few plays by the controversial playwright.

Movie director Fritz Lang then offered him the part of the possessed murderer in "M."

In 1933, Hitler became chancellor of Germany with full dictatorial powers. Peter joined a number of Jewish artists who caught trains for Paris, carrying no baggage.

Alfred Hitchcock invited Peter to London in 1934, offering him the part of the foreign terrorist in "The Man Who Knew Too Much." Not knowing English, Peter memorized the dialogue, hardly understanding it fully but guided by his intuition.

Hollywood beckoned, with mostly parts of a homicidal maniac in horror films like "Mad Love."

His attempt to exercise control over the course of his professional life failed when his pet project—the portrayal of Raskolnikov in Dostoevsky's "Crime and Punishment"—was perceived as merely another horror movie.

Now and then Lorre managed to get a plum part. Among his notable achievements were the characterizations of Mr. Moto, the Oriental detective, in a series of low-budget movies; Joel Cairo, the effeminate gunsel of "The Maltese Falcon," the first of a number of thrillers that united him with Humphrey Bogart and Sidney Greenstreet; Dr. Einstein, the drunken plastic surgeon of the zany "Arsenic and Old Lace."

Unfortunately, Lorre found himself mostly in pictures that stifled his creative juices. He tried to make light of the situation, preserving a sense of fun and pranks on the set, but following his abrupt death of a cerebral hemorrhage in 1946, it was recognized that, tragically, a major talent had fizzled steadily to a point of travesty.

The Films of Peter Lorre brings back nostalgic, high and low memories. In additional to biographical data, the book contains casts, credits and synopses of Lorre's entire movie canon. Hundreds of photographs illustrate the text.

It is a worthy, long overdue epitaph. (Amnon Kabatchnik)

James Lee Burke. *Neon Rain*. Henry Holt, 1987.
James Lee Burke. *Heaven's Prisoners*. Henry Holt, 1988.

It has become commonplace in the world of hard-boiled fiction for a new writer to be ballyhooed as the new Hammett, Chandler, or Macdonald, but most of these writers really provide little more than a rehash of the same tired formula of sex, fast guns, and tough-guy witticisms.

Knowing that, it is a particular pleasure to read the first two volumes of a projected trilogy by Southern novelist James Lee Burke. Burke is a college professor and successful mainstream novelist and short-story writer who has formerly written such critically acclaimed work as *The Convict* and *The Lost Get-Back Boogie*. Burke has a well-developed knack for writing poetically and compellingly about rugged, proletarian characters, and it was probably foreordained that he would one day turn his talents to the hard-boiled crime novel.

Burke's character is Dave Robicheaux, an alcoholic, jazz buff, and New Orleans homicide detective. Robicheaux is a complicated figure, having survived a failed marriage to a society beauty and the depredations of the bottle. He is a sad man who has become something of a pragmatist, yet he retains a touching idealism that leavens his cynicism.

In this first outing, *Neon Rain,* Robicheaux makes a grim trip to Angola prison to make a final visit to a condemned convict. The man warns him that a Central American drug kingpin in New Orleans has put out a contract on him. It seems that Dave is paying too much attention to the death of a young black prostitute whose needle-pocked body he found in a backwoods bayou.

Before the story has progressed much further, Dave's unwillingness to sweep the case under the rug and his propensity for meeting trouble head-on catapults him into a struggle involving Mafia chieftains, half-crazed mer-

cenaries, crooked cops, and a retired general who is med-
dling in Central American politics.

Burke has strengthened a familiar story with elements
that make it unusual. Constantly threatened by his own
self-destructiveness, Dave never quite gives in to the
inner torments that constantly threaten to turn him into
a worthless drunk. Dave's idealism runs counter to that
in many detectives in that it is a weakness rather than a
strength. Often it forces him, against all convention wis-
dom, to risk far too much in order to see justice done.

Burke portrays violence well, both physical and
psychological. He allows scenes of physical violence to
come out in short, sharp, uncontrolled bursts that
emphasize the inability of a man to do anything but react
when faced with death. Burke's understanding of
psychological violence is especially good. Burke, like
Elmore Leonard and John D. MacDonald, has a strong
sense that the fear of violence can often be worse than
the violence itself.

Burke also rivals Elmore Leonard in his depiction of
female characters. In Annie Ballard, Burke has created a
believable female heroine who is brave without being violent. Her resiliency protects her from the dangers
inherent in her relationship with Dave and ultimately
saves Dave himself from his own inner demons.

In *Heaven's Prisoners,* Burke picks up Dave's life after
he has retired form the New Orleans Police Department.
Married to Annie, he now runs a bait shop and charter
service in New Iberia, Louisiana. While fishing in the Gulf
with Annie, he sees a plane go down and arrives in time
to save only one person, a tiny Central American girl,
from the wreck. This purely accidental occurrence once
again involves him with drug runners and federal
duplicity. His unwillingness to mind his own business
brings the full wrath of the criminals down on his head
and his peaceful life is shattered forever.

Burke is an unusual writer of crime stories in that he
is willing to take genuine risks with his characters. Dave
soaks up the requisite physical punishment in the course
of these two stories, but the emotional damage he is
forced to endure is so realistically and graphically
depicted that the reader will come away from it visibly
shaken. The third and final chapter in Dave's life is due
to appear late in 1988 or early in 1989, and this writer
unhesitatingly recommends it sight unseen. (Bob Skinner)

O'Neill De Noux. *Grim Reaper.* Zebra Books, 1988.

A new and unusual entry on the crime scene is the debut of O'Neill De Noux, a former New Orleans homicide detective and a real-life private investigator. In *Grim Reaper,* De Noux tells the story of a deranged sex killer who stalks the streets of the French Quarter and the Garden District as he preys upon attractive young women.

De Noux's hero is Dino La Stanza, a newly promoted homicide detective. As he tells the story in the first person, La Stanza and his partner track the killer from murder scene to murder scene until the pieces of the puzzle come together to produce the solution.

The story takes us into fairly familiar territory with its deranged sex-maniac killer and the young detective who must manage his own personal problems while coping with the demands of an urgent investigation. However, De Noux manages to keep the story from degenerating into trite formula with the realism he brings to the investigation itself.

De Noux is clearly a student of the Wambaugh school of crime fiction. His cops exude an adolescent quality as they play grab-ass and make bad jokes at the scenes of gruesome murders. However, the surreal horror that De Noux evokes as he describes a murder scene makes it clear that the horsing around is the working cop's way of staying sane when confronted with dismembered corpses and pools of blood. At the same time, his cops are thorough-going professionals who leaven their foolishness with a clear understanding of the kind of criminal they are dealing with.

De Noux is also to be praised for not having the story wind up with another chase scene or a blazing gun battle. There is little cop-perpetrated violence in *Grim Reaper* and some may find the resolution somewhat anticlimactic, but students of true crime are well aware that real murder investigations consist of endlessly going over picayune detail until a pattern or a positive solution emerges.

The story has a few problems. La Stanza, following in the footsteps of many other tough hero, has a past, but De Noux tells far too much about it and resolves it far too easily.

Other problems also are evident in the hero's love life. The degeneration of a love affair with a working-class girlfriend is handled rather well and, knowing what we know about the break-up rate of police marriages and love affairs, rings true to life. A subsequent love affair between La Stanza and the wealthy sister of a murder victim is rather predictable and lacks credibility.

Readers should also beware if they are offended by strong language. *Grim Reaper,* written in a hyper-realistic vein, is *very* salty.

As a first novel, however, *Grim Reaper* is a good effort. It provides a realistic look at a homicide investigation and also at the personalities of the kind of men who undertake such work in our era. (Bob Skinner)

MYSTERY MOSTS: COMIC BOOK HEROES AGAIN

Not surprisingly, with respect to length of career in years, the crime fighting heroes of the comic books hold to much the same pattern as they do in number of books. But there are some divergences. *Superman* comics will complete a half century in Summer 1989. (Yes, there was some celebration of "Superman's Fiftieth Birthday" in 1987, but that dated from his original appearance in *Action* comics.) *Batman* comics will be fifty years old in early 1990. Charlie Chan was around in *The Adventures of Charlie Chan* twice (1948-49 and 1955-56), with Dell's *Charlie Chan* running concurrently with the latter, and in *The New Adventures of Charlie Chan* (1958-59) and *The Amazing Chan and the Chan Clan* (1973-74), for a total comicbook existence of eight years. *The Saint* was published over a six-year span by Avon. All pretty much as you would expect.

The Divergences mentioned? *The Shadow* and *Doc Savage* are closer in total years (sixteen and eight, respectively) than in total number of issues. That shift is largely due to the fact that neither of them would have had a comics revival without Bantam's ongoing revival of the Doc novels, so that during the revival years it was the Man of Bronze and not the Old Mind Clouder who was the more important.

The biggest change is that Dick Tracy, trailing Superman by more than three to one in issues (and Batman by almost as much) has a more respectable years-to-years ratio. His two McKay years were followed by eleven with Dell, then twelve more with Harvey, for a total of twenty-five. Superman won't be two-to-one ahead in number of issues until 1989. (Jeff Banks)

The Documents in the Case
(Letters)

From Douglas G. Greene, 627 New Hampshire Avenue, Norfolk, VA 23508:

John Dickson Carr's widow has authorized me to write a biography of JDC, and she and John's relatives are supplying information. I think that the book will be quire informative, for I already have a good amount of unrecorded material. But I need the help of all Carr fans far and wide (and near and narrow, as well). Anyone who knew John, or who corresponded with him, or who has autographed copies of his books (his inscriptions often say something interesting about the book) is invited to contact me.

From Ben Fisher, Box 816, University, MS 38677:

The revamped TMF looks great, and the items published in the new issue [10:1] look interesting. Long ago, in Ellery Queen's *To the Queen's Taste,* an announcement about publishing a previously unpublished manuscript story by "Clifford Ashdown" was made. I can't discover that that piece ever appeared--at least not in EQMM, where, according to the notice, it was to appear. Anyone out there have information regarding this?

By the way, since I'm teaching classes in detective fiction in alternate years, I thought you'd like to know that students repeatedly come to me singing the praises of Walter Albert's bibliography, from Brownstone.

From Kathy Phillips, 364 Main St., North Andover, MA
01845:

I enjoyed Volume 10 #2 very much, every bit as much
as the preceding #1, and I am delighted that Mr. Deeck
has been elevated and expanded. *[You make him sound
like a hot-air balloon!]* His reviews are priceless—which
I suppose means that he can't sell them separately and
may as well give them to you. He is a wonderful writer
and must be a charming, amusing friend. *[He is, indeed.]*
Thanks for his company.

But with you I have a bone to pick:

In your response to Mr. Fellows' letter (his homo-
phobia surprised me—I always thought Australians were
pretty much "live-and-let-live" people) you say, "I
dislike Josephine Tey not because of her sexual proclivities, real or imagined, which are none of my business,
but because of her intellectual dishonesty, which *is* my
business." Why? I mean, after all, she wrote a mystery
novel, didn't she, *not* a learned historical treatise.
Intellectual dishonesty? A bit strong, don't you think?
To Prove a Villain is much better as history, no question,
but I think *The Daughter of Time* works very well as
fiction (you know, as in "imaginary").

Some very good popular books have been written, e.g.
The Murder of the Man Who Was Shakespeare, which
promulgate the proposition that someone other than
Shakespeare (Marlowe, Bacon, Devereaux) wrote the
sublime works for which he was given credit. *I* think the
proposition is so much nonsense, and those books which
purport to be the final and complete statement on the
subject (and lack all humor) may be intellectually dishonest as well. But some of the books are entertaining,
everyone is entitled to his/her opinion, that's what makes
horse races, and the books sometimes make good mysteries *as fiction*.

I have no trouble with your disagreeing with her
methods (as an [sic] historian, which she wasn't) or with
her conclusions (she *was* probably wrong as it happens),
but I don't think casting aspersions on her intellectual
honesty is quite fair in the context of the woman's life or
her craft. Anyway, don't you think that your Tey-
bashing is getting old? Tey wrote some fine books—
novels, *fiction*—that continue to be read and enjoyed long
after her death. That's what she was about. Leave her
be already.

[(1) The truth is everybody's business, and the person who acquiesces in a lie is as much a liar as the person who tells it.   (2) Tey deliberately maligned a profession which is no less honorable than any other, and certainly no less honorable than the legal profession, to which you and I both belong; historians as a group are neither liars, fools, nor knaves—all three of which Tey, at one time or another in her book, accuses them of being. (3) Tey herself was so dishonest that she ignored all evidence which contravened her position, distorted any evidence which could be twisted so as to appear to support her position, and resorted to every logical fallacy ever invented to promote her patently false revisionist version of history.   (4) She was a plagiarist, and an ungrateful one at that; she not only stole every one of her Richardist ideas from the noted humbug Sir Clements Markham (given Sir Clements' own "sexual proclivities," perhaps I should have said "the noted humbugger"), but she dismissed his contributions [sic] contemptuously. (5) She was, not to put too fine a point on it, a deliberate liar, and deliberate liars deserved to be bashed regularly and enthusiastically.   Even so, I'll be happy to stop "bashing" Tey just as soon as her supporters stop trying to sell her claptrap as The Truth.

[To my way of thinking, Ms. Tey was not a very pleasant person.   Nor, from my limited contact with her writings, am I inclined to agree with your evidently high regard for her as a mystery writer.   The only other work of hers that I ever tried to read was The Man in the Queue, which contains in a single paragraph two of the dumbest ideas in the history of literature: "In [Inspector Grant's] opinion the man had been stabbed a considerable time—perhaps ten minutes or more—before he had collapsed as the people in front moved away.   In a squash like that he would be held up and moved along by the crowd.   In fact, it would have been a sheer impossibility to fall if one had wanted to in such a closely packed mob. He thought it highly unlikely that the man was even aware that he had been struck.   So much pressing and squeezing and involuntary hurting went on on these occasions that a sudden and not too painful blow would not be noticed."   Multiple-choice question: Who is the most stupid—(a) the people in line, for propping up and carrying along a corpse for ten minutes without knowing it was a corpse; (b) the dead man himself, for not noticing that he had been struck a death blow; (c) Inspector

Grant, for thinking that people in line would carry a corpse along for ten minutes without knowing it was a corpse and for thinking that the dead man wouldn't even have noticed that he had been struck a death blow; (d) Tey, for writing this crap; or (d) the reading public, for buying it.

[To put it as delicately as possible, Tey was a turkey.]

From William F. Deeck, 9020 Autoville Drive, College Park, MD 20740:

Hey, wait a minute, Guy! You never asked for a column of my short reviews, which I'm sure you are aware are nonexistent. Marv Lachman is the master of the less-is-more school, and Andy Jaysnovitch is continuing the good work. I am a proponent of the too—much—is—never—enough school.

To forestall or at least tie Charlie Shibuk as he dashes in with the news, I recently discovered that there was another U.S. publication of Jonathan Latimer's The Fifth Grave—by Mercury Mystery Jonathan Press J65, abridged. I've never seen a copy, but it was advertised in one of the Mercury books I have. It would be interesting to make a comparison of the texts.

Even more interesting would be a comparison with the original British publication. Failing that, Steve Stilwell recently advertised a signed, limited—edition reprint of *Solomon's Vineyard,* the original title, which I would imagine is taken from the English edition. The $125 price, however, curbed my craving for exegesis.

My interest in the detective pulps was minimal. When pulps were still being published, I read the science-fiction ones. Recently, however, I have been dipping into some of the anthologies and am finding that, selectively, the stories are fun reading. So I encourage Bob Sampson in his efforts to inform us about those stories and hope that Otto Penzler is making notes for future Mysterious Library publications.

My thanks for the further info about investigations into the paranormal. Obviously I have not been keeping up with the field, as my reliance on Charles Fort would seem to indicate.

Index to The Mystery Fancier
Volume 8
January-June 1984
July-December 1986
Compiled by Williams F. Deeck

Notes: The number preceding the slash is the issue number; the number or numbers after the slash are the page numbers. (R) equals reviews; (IAC) reviews in It's About Crime; (MS) comments or reviews in "Mysteriously Speaking..."; (L:) Letter, the contents of which have not been indexed. Book titles are in caps; short stories, films, and television shows are quoted. Alphabetization is by the Word Perfect sort program, which has its own way of doing things, with an occasional refinement. If what you're looking for isn't precisely where you would expect it to be, look up or down a few items and just maybe—